THE TRANSFORMATIVE JOURNEY OF HIGHER EDUCATION IN PRISON

This volume follows one man's revolutionary journey from deficient early education to his incarceration on North Carolina's death row, where he was given the opportunity to pursue higher education.

By pairing Lyle May's engaging first-person account with current scholarly literature, this book examines the complex relationship between the United States' educational and penal systems. It also documents the role of education in May's contributions to society through writing, teaching, and activism. Flouting the stereotype that people sentenced to long prison terms lack an ability or desire for higher education, May's experience champions individualism as a means of overcoming most environmental challenges to learning, personal growth, and societal involvement. With the right amount of motivation and dedication, even prison walls do not preclude significant contributions to the community or participation in criminal justice reform. Granting access to higher education in places that often lack an academic apparatus, Ohio University's College Program for the Incarcerated provides an avenue for correctional students to enroll in accredited correspondence courses and earn an Associate or Bachelors of Specialized Studies degree. This book's recounting of May's experience with the program augments existing literature on higher education in prison by illustrating the tragic but common pitfall of the school-to-prison pipeline and one man's determination to pursue higher education despite the hindrances inherent in the prison environment.

Informing both students and educators about aspects of prison life that are not always considered, this book is a valuable component of a well-rounded corrections course reading list. It is essential for educators and students, criminal justice reformers, criminologists, penologists, or any reader intent on understanding how independent learning is critical to unlocking the rehabilitative and reintegrative potential of higher education in prison.

Lyle C. May is an Ohio University alum, member of the Alpha Sigma Lambda Honor Society, incarcerated journalist, advocate for higher education, and activist. He recently published the book *Witness: An Insider's Narrative of the Carceral State.*

Amanda K. Cox is an Associate Professor of Instruction in the Department of Sociology and Anthropology at Ohio University and is an affiliate of the university's Center for Law, Justice, and Culture. She was a recipient of the Dr. Eric A. Wagner Endowed Professorship and Ohio University Honors Tutorial College Distinguished Mentor Award in 2022. She teaches undergraduate and graduate courses in sociology and criminology, taking a sociological approach to the study of criminological theory, the death penalty, ethics in law and justice, and crime and media. Dr. Cox's research interests include the death penalty, racial and socioeconomic inequality in punishment, ethics in law and justice, and criminological theory. Her research has been published in several academic journals.

Lisa M. Carter is an Associate Professor of Criminology at Florida Southern College. She also teaches courses for the Women and Gender Studies program. She earned her B.A. in Sociology from the University of Kentucky, and her M.S. in Corrections and Juvenile Justice Studies from Eastern Kentucky University. She completed her Ph.D. in Criminology at Indiana University of Pennsylvania. Her research interests include female criminality, corrections and rehabilitation, reintegration, and death penalty issues. She is the co-editor of the books, *Female Offenders and Reentry: Pathways and Barriers to Returning to Society* (Routledge, 2018) and *Punishing Gender Past and Present: Examining the Criminal Justice System across Gendered Experiences*. Dr. Carter co-authored the second edition of *The Decision-Making Network: An Introduction to Criminal Justice*. Additionally, she has published in *Corrections: Policy, Practice, and Research*, *Violence and Victims*, and *Journal of Homosexuality*. She holds professional memberships with the Academy of Criminal Justice Sciences, American Society of Criminology, and Southwestern Social Sciences Association. She is a supporter of the Pennsylvania Prison Society and Pace Center for Girls.

THE TRANSFORMATIVE JOURNEY OF HIGHER EDUCATION IN PRISON

A Class of One

Lyle C. May
with Amanda K. Cox and Lisa M. Carter

Routledge
Taylor & Francis Group

NEW YORK AND LONDON

Designed cover image: © Getty Images

First published 2025
by Routledge
605 Third Avenue, New York, NY 10158

and by Routledge
4 Park Square, Milton Park, Abingdon, Oxon OX14 4RN

Routledge is an imprint of the Taylor & Francis Group, an informa business

© 2025 Lyle C. May, Amanda K. Cox, and Lisa M. Carter

Library of Congress Cataloging-in-Publication Data
Names: May, Lyle C., author. | Cox, Amanda K., editor. |
Carter, Lisa M., editor.
Title: The transformative journey of higher education in prison : a class of one / Lyle C. May ; edited by Amanda K. Cox and Lisa M. Carter.
Description: New York, NY : Routledge, 2024. | Includes bibliographical references and index.
Identifiers: LCCN 2024006772 (print) | LCCN 2024006773 (ebook) |
ISBN 9781032582894 (hardback) | ISBN 9781032582870 (paperback) |
ISBN 9781003449454 (ebook)
Subjects: LCSH: May, Lyle C. | Prisoners--Education (Higher)--North
Carolina--Biography.
Classification: LCC HV8883.3.U52 .N863 2024 (print) | LCC HV8883.3.U52
(ebook) | DDC 365/.666092 [B]--dc23/eng/20240423
LC record available at https://lccn.loc.gov/2024006772
LC ebook record available at https://lccn.loc.gov/2024006773

ISBN: 978-1-032-58289-4 (hbk)
ISBN: 978-1-032-58287-0 (pbk)
ISBN: 978-1-003-44945-4 (ebk)

DOI: 10.4324/9781003449454

Typeset in Sabon
by Taylor & Francis Books

This book is dedicated to everyone on the inside who seeks to learn, but lacks the opportunity; and to Fr. Dan Kenna, who answered when I knocked.

CONTENTS

ACKNOWLEDGEMENTS

Becoming a vocal advocate for higher education in prison, and writing a book about how valuable it is, would not have been possible without the support of many friends, mentors, and scholars. Many thanks go to:

Dr. Amanda Cox, for urging me to write this book, typing and editing chapters as I sent them, taking a chance on me, inviting me to speak with her students about my experiences in the criminal legal system, instructing me in advanced criminology, and helping bring this project to completion. You are easily my favorite Ohio University professor.

Dr. Lisa Carter, for all the editing, typing and work on the citations, coordination with Dr. Cox, contact with Ellen Boyne at Routledge, and for inviting me to talk with your students about my experiences in the criminal legal system. It was providential that you bumped into Ellen at the annual American Society of Criminology Conference to discuss our proposal.

Kyle McKenzie, the best academic advisor on the continent. Your counsel advanced my higher education and academic potential in ways that continue to bear fruit. Ohio University is lucky to have you, and any student that has you as an advisor will benefit from your guidance.

Tara Kumar, for always encouraging me, staying by my side throughout my incarceration, and handling many of the things in this process I cannot.

Thank you, Charlotte West for expanding my understanding of Prison Education Programs, federal funding, and demonstrating that some journalists genuinely care about people in prison. Your reporting on higher education in prison is an invaluable resource.

Thank you, Ginny Cotrill, for inducting me into the Alpha Sigma Lambda Honor Society's psi delta chapter at Ohio University.

Thank you, Dr. Frank Baumgartner for giving me my first invitation to speak with a university class. Your support and instruction have been critical in my academic journey.

A special thanks to the many professors and instructors who have invited me to share my experiences in the criminal legal system with their classes. Your acceptance of me, and your students' engaged questions, helped me grow in ways I could not have fathomed:

Seth Kotch—UNC Chapel Hill; Robert Johnson—American University; Marhta Hurley—Dayton University; Bernard Harcourt—Columbia University; Julie Stone-Peters—Columbia University; Alexis Hoag-Forjuor—Brooklyn Law School; Carolyn Hoyle—Oxford University; Josh Page—University of Minnesota at Minneapolis; Esther Mathews—Gonzaga University; Brittany Ripper—Marymount College; Paulo Barrazo—Boston College; Barbara Zaitow—Appalachian State University; Will Hummel—The Dalton School; Donald Little—Wake Tech Community College; and Buff Easterly—Mount St. Mary's Academy High School.

Thanks to Ellen Boyne at Routledge Academic Press for helping make the publication of this a book a reality.

Thank you to the Catholic Community of St. Francis of Assisi in Raleigh, North Carolina for all of their support.

Finally, thank you mom and dad for teaching me to be fearless in all of my pursuits, and for always believing in me.

Editors Amanda K. Cox and Lisa M. Carter would like to thank student workers at Ohio University and Florida Southern College for their help typing chapters for this book. Special thanks to Ohio University Honors Tutorial College graduate Sydney Borsellino, sociology graduate student Katie Weingard and Florida Southern undergraduate student Kyla Strength.

FOREWORD

Being a professor is a gift of lifelong learning. With each passing semester as an Associate Professor of Instruction at Ohio University, I have the privilege of continuing my development as a sociologist, criminologist, and educator. When I taught my first course at Indiana University of Pennsylvania in 2008, I could not have imagined how essential education would become to my identity nor how enlightening and inspiring working with students would be. My students teach and challenge me each time I step into the classroom. They are my teachers as much as I am theirs. But not all teaching and learning happens inside the classroom, and my experience working with Lyle May has reinforced that learning and personal development can and does happen, not only outside of the classroom, but in the least conducive of places and despite significant obstacles.

I met Lyle in 2018 during my first year of teaching in Ohio University's Department of Sociology and Anthropology. As a student of the university's print-based correctional education program, which was developed in 1974, Lyle had seen my sociology capstone course, *The Death Penalty in the United States*, in the course catalog and asked his academic advisor to put us in touch. The first time we talked on the phone, Lyle expressed his interest in becoming a guest speaker in my capstone course. For him, this was an opportunity to talk with other students about the criminal legal system, the challenges and gifts of his own education, and to confront long-standing narratives about people on death row. For me and the dozens of students with whom Lyle has since spoken in my classes, his involvement has given us the chance to critique the criminal legal system through the lens of a person who understands it experientially and academically. Since the first time Lyle spoke in my capstone course, he has given guest lectures in one of my classes each semester, inspiring students to challenge colloquial claims about the utility and ethics of death as punishment. In one of our discussions outside of the classroom, I suggested to Lyle that his experience, education, and talent for writing could extend his reach beyond prison walls and even college classrooms. This is when the idea for this book was born, and Lyle started writing. As part of this process, Lyle and I collaborated on an independent study in advanced criminological theory that culminated in the academic essays that introduce each section of this book. The completed volume that you hold in your hands (or see on your screen) are evidence that, despite the barriers he faces in prison, Lyle continues to grow as a learner and as an educator.

As Lyle explains throughout this book, prison is a place where restriction is standard and support for growth, whether educational or personal, is scarce. As my student and collaborator, Lyle taught me about perseverance when his coursework was disrupted by administrative choices, and he refused to give up his right to higher education. He taught me about intellectual curiosity each time we discussed scholarly work for his independent study, posing questions that challenged me to think more deeply about ideas I took for granted during my own formal education. Most importantly, he taught me, as so many of my students do, that I still have so much to learn about what it means to teach and be educated. By reading this book, students of sociology, criminology, and criminal justice will be encouraged to confront their beliefs about education for incarcerated people and the wisdom of investing in a prison system that, by its very design, blocks earnest attempts at education and reform.

Amanda K. Cox, Ph.D.

PART 1

The School-to-Prison Pipeline

Juvenile delinquency is generally defined as criminal acts committed by persons under the age of eighteen. This definition does not include youth who are charged and tried as adults. In most jurisdictions of the United States, juveniles are viewed through a different lens in the criminal legal system because they lack a full capacity to understand the long-term consequences of their behavior, and because they are more susceptible to rehabilitation. A more nuanced discussion of adolescent brain development will be laid out in the next section. Part 1 is an examination of pathways to incarceration for juveniles, or the school-to-prison pipeline.

There is no single comprehensive theory or picture of what causes juveniles to commit delinquent acts. There are, however, common sociocultural and social interactive factors in the home and school environments. Foremost among them are peer influence and one's valuation of a particular set of goals. Whose goals and why are key questions sociological theories seek to answer with varying degrees of effectiveness.

Sociologist Albert K. Cohen (1955) suggested that lower-class youth internalize the goals of middle-class culture but experience "status frustration," or internal psychological distress over the inability to attain those goals. The American class system, claimed Cohen (1955), determines middleclass values and norms children are expected to strive for and achieve:

> There norms are, in effect, a tempered version of the Protestant ethic which has played such an important part in shaping American character and American society ... this middleclass ethic prescribes an obligation to

DOI: 10.4324/9781003449454-1

strive, by dint of rational ascetic, self-discipline, and independent activity, to achieve in worldly affairs.

(p. 87)

One's "status" in school is measured by middle-class standards. The first job of the teacher is to instill American values and promote the development of middle-class personalities amongst students. It is here the battle over what that means in a historical context is fiercest: such as white conservative politicians who oppose teaching students evolution and Critical Race Theory in public schools. Generally, teachers are likely to be middle-class people who value these virtues in students at the expense of those who fail to display such virtues.

Cohen (1955) pointed out the educational system itself favors "quiet, cooperative, 'well-behaved' pupils" who enable instruction, and the institution actively rejects students "who are destructive of order, routine, and predictability in the classroom" (as cited in Bartollas & Schmalleger, 2014, pp. 90 & 103). Cohen (1955) defined nine norms of the middle-class measuring rod: 1) ambition, 2) individual responsibility, 3) achievement, 4) temperance, 5) rationality, 6) courtesy and likeability, 7) lowered physical aggression, 8) educational recreation, and 9) respect for property.

Feeling that middle-class goals like achievement or temperance are unattainable, and failing to reach them, the youth experiences "status frustration." To lessen this strain, he or she becomes defiant and hostile toward unattainable goals. They act out in class or seek like-minded peers who engage in a subculture (e.g., gang) that openly rejects and replaces middle-class values through delinquent acts or continues to pursue those goals through unconventional means.

Beyond socioeconomic status, social theorists believe cold and brittle relationships, ostracism, and low levels of attachment to friends increase the likelihood of delinquency. Greater attachment to parents, church, school, and similar conventional institutions reduces the likelihood of delinquency (Akers et al., 2017). Leading social control theorist Travis Hirschi emphasized the fact that parental attachment is important in the maintenance of conformity, but it did not matter to whom one is attached. Attachment is better than weak bonds, even if the person is a poor model of behavior (Akers et al., 2017).

Holding delinquency (or worthiness) of friends truly constant at any level, the more one respects or admires one's friends, the less likely one is to commit delinquent acts. We honor those we admire not by imitation, but by adherence to conventional standards.

(Akers et al., 2017, p. 174)

After attachment, commitment, involvement, and belief are links to the maintenance of strong bonds. The greater one's commitment to education, the more likely one is to succeed. Less commitment makes conformity to social norms less likely, and delinquent acts easier to rationalize (Akers et al., 2017). Hirschi (1969) believed a youth's involvement in conventional activities like study, family time, and extracurricular activities creates a preoccupation with conventional pursuits instead of deviant ones. However, social bonds require belief or the endorsement of conventional values and norms versus unconventional ones. "The less a person believes he should obey the rules, the more likely he is to violate them" (p. 26).

Academic achievement, which is usually defined by test scores, grades, and self-perception of academic activities, is indicative of the strength of a student's bond to school. Attachment is measured by a positive attitude toward school, concern for teacher opinions, and acceptance of the school's authority (Akers et al., 2017). If a youth perceives academic achievement as an unattainable goal, the attachment is weakened. Any premature engagement in adult activities, such as smoking, drinking, drug use, sexual intercourse, or teen pregnancy, indicates a lesser commitment to educational goals. Neglecting homework and study, social isolation, and not engaging in extracurricular activities demonstrate a measurable lack of involvement and belief in conventional values, making it more likely one commits delinquent acts, but not making it a certainty.

School is about more than building social bonds. Youth spend as much time in school as the average adult working forty hours a week, learning as much in the classroom as they do from peers. Contrary to Hirschi's (1969) findings, conventional friends foster conventional behaviors, but unconventional friends encourage delinquent ones. Differential association theorists have maintained that delinquency is a behavior learned through social interaction with peers who have internalized a preponderance of definitions conductive to low violations (Sutherland, 1956, pp. 7–29).

While being socialized at school, students are adversely impacted by prisonized learning environments, those that micromanage student behavior and are more punitive than other schools. Students are also negatively impacted by prisonized schools designed to appear and function as punitive, restrictive environments that regulate the smallest details. The crime control model is the guiding principle in many urban public schools, with uniformed guards, metal detectors, random locker searches, drug sniffing dogs, silent alarms for teachers, and student ID cards to get in locked classrooms (Payne & Welch, 2010).

Students considered "troublesome" in these draconian environments are sometimes labeled "suspects" under "investigation," or "repeat offenders" subjected to "interrogation" and "detainment" if they have been disciplined before. As a result of this law enforcement language and labeling, minority students are targeted by SROs and often receive more detentions, suspensions, and expulsions. The school-to-prison pipeline construct (STPP) "purports that exclusionary discipline enacts a series of events that stigmatizes and pushes students out of school and into [the] justice system" (Pesta, 2018).

Deviant labels contribute to delinquent behaviors and identities, but research suggests it also limits future educational achievement and economic mobility. Across racial minority populations these deficits and disadvantages are the most pronounced (Pesta, 2018). Ethno-racial minorities also experience mere exclusionary discipline because of labeling and have fewer resources to cope (Pesta, 2018). Though Black and Hispanic youth have the highest rates of exclusionary discipline, Hispanic and white youth have the highest level of delinquency (Pesta, 2018). This is due, in part, to the belief that white and affluent youth are protected from the negative impact of delinquent labels, have access to more resources, and often receive more lenient treatment from the criminal legal system (Pesta, 2018). Where "white privilege" might lead to a diversion program such as drug rehab for a white youth caught with a small amount of marijuana, Black youth are disproportionately incarcerated for the same behavior (Pesta, 2018).

School failure and drop out are directly linked to socialization with delinquent peers and labeling by teachers or other school officials. School failure can, in turn, create psychological problems in youth such as low self-esteem and self-efficacy, the coping mechanism for which is often substance use. School failure and delinquency also share common factors such as poverty, family dysfunction, and gang involvement. Though the school as an institution is the arbiter of adolescent values, it fails to recognize these values vary across class and race, underserving minority populations and contributing to the STPP.

It is important to emphasize that within the nexus of school failure, delinquent culture, and the STPP is the critical influence of tobacco, alcohol, and illicit substances like marijuana. Substance use by adolescents in school or recreationally is a means to an end, such as achieving excitement and easing social interaction. Substance use—especially tobacco, alcohol, and marijuana—can promote exploration of new social spheres, sexual relationships, and unfamiliar circumstances (Bartollas & Schmalleger, 2014).

Users may begin smoking and drinking to relieve stress and anxiety, but when more dangerous, highly addictive substances are used to cope, their damaging effects can have a lasting impact on the youth's life. Substance use becomes abuse when the user's behavior is dysfunctional-the youth struggles to perform in or attend school, maintain social or family bonds, exhibits reckless or dangerous behaviors, and commits crimes to support their habit. Dependency, either drug addiction or alcoholism, weakens social bonds and might begin as a minor delinquent act for a youth but can quickly escalate to more serious crimes to continue "getting high."

Kandel and Yamaguchi (1993) utilized cross sectional research and long-itudinal data and proposed a developmental model for drug use involvement. From their findings they proposed that alcohol use follows a pattern of minor delinquency and exposure to peers who drink; marijuana can follow or precede minor delinquency and adoption of unconventional beliefs and values opposed by parents and teachers, but consistent with unconventional peers; adolescent drug use escalates with continued exposure to more illicit substances and crim-inal activity, leading to exclusionary discipline, drop out, and arrest.

Substance abuse may develop in youths who exhibit common social/ environmental risk factors (Bartollas & Schmalleger, 2014). For example, a family history of alcoholism increases the likelihood an adolescent will also abuse alcohol. A genetic predisposition or addiction-prone personality can increase the likelihood of substance abuse. The emotionality of hormonal development in adolescence, combined with the pressure of an academic environment, can increase stress to a degree that "partying" becomes a see-mingly innocuous form of relief, but individuals already struggling acade-mically may find this slippery slope leads to failure and a cycle of substance abuse. Substance abuse is also a learned behavior that begins with observa-tion and initiation of certain behaviors like binge drinking, continues with social reinforcement or encouragement by peers, and culminates in an ado-lescent's expectation of positive social, psychological, and physiological consequences from habitual substance use (Bartollas & Schmalleger, 2014)

Underage drinking at a party is a form of gateway delinquency, that may lead to more serious types of substance use and criminal activities later on. Hagan (1991) integrated drift theory-the idea juveniles neutralize the moral hold of society and "drift" into increasingly delinquent behavior-with social control theory as a life course conceptualization of delinquency. Hagan (1991) found:

> adolescents adrift from parental and educational control are more likely than those with more controls to develop mild or more seriously deviant subculture preferences [and that] among males with working class origins identification with the subculture of delinquency has a negative effect on trajectories of early adult status attainments.
>
> *(as cited in Bartollas & Schmalleger, 2014, p. 113)*

Adolescents who have weak bonds to family and school are more likely to struggle academically, abuse substances, suffer from underlying mental health problems, interact with delinquent peers, engage in delinquent behavior, experience exclusionary discipline at school, and drop out. Lacking a high school diploma, or just having a GED (the "equivalent" of a tenth-grade education), significantly limits earning potential. Dropouts comprise nearly half of all households on welfare. Dropouts also comprise over half of the nation's incarcerated population (Pesta, 2018).

Whether youth enter the STPP through a substance abuse-specific pathway, or one marked by systematic racism, that same variation determines whether a youth receives a diversion program or is incarcerated. One of the more detestable parts of this process is the disproportionality of minority youth confinement. In the juvenile justice system, Black youths are more likely to receive harsher punishments and more often waived into the adult criminal justice system than White youths (Campaign for Youth Justice, 2012). Disproportionality is a trend that can be traced from exclusionary discipline in school, through policing of urban minority communities and arrest rates, and into youth detention centers, jails, and prisons.

For those youth who do not receive access to diversion programs such as probation, substance abuse treatment, or alternative dispute resolution (restorative justice) as first-time offenders, states differ in how they adjudicate anyone under eighteen at the time of the crime. The line between juvenile and adult adjudication is blurred in most states. Over 12,000 life sentences have been imposed on individuals under the age of eighteen (Mover & Nelis, 2018). Every state, except Maine and West Virginia, confine adolescents sentenced to life imprisonment for crimes that range from drug and property offenses to robbery, aggravated assault, sexual assault, and homicide (Mover & Nelis, 2018). Children as young as ten years old have been sentenced to die in prison, casualties of tough-on-crime policies of the 1980s and 1990s that implemented mandatory minimums, three-strikes laws, and liberal use of life without parole. This same tough-on-crime philosophy also undermined the effectiveness of juvenile and adult corrections.

What works in juvenile detention centers, training schools, and reformatories is not typically what occurs. Effective rehabilitative methodologies treat the underlying problems that prompted the delinquent behavior. Psychotherapeutic programming such as insight-based therapies address faulty or unconventional thinking, group therapies can address negative peer influence, and substance abuse intervention can disrupt the cycle with 12 Step Programs. Basic education and GED testing occur, but there is insufficient access to higher education or transitional vocation-to-job programs.

The dominant correctional model for youth is "crime control." This model mirrors the adult penal system and supports discipline and punishment as the remedy for juvenile delinquency. A punishment-centered philosophy promotes the severity and certainty of the sentence and greater reliance on incarceration. A fundamental assumption of the crime control model is that unlawful behavior is a character defect that can be "corrected" through confinement; that punishment teaches responsibility, diligence, and honesty; and that "deterrence of youth crime depends on the juvenile justice system apprehending and punishing youthful offenders with greater speed, efficacy, and certainty" (Bartollas & Schmalleger, 2014, p. 310). Like David Fodel' " justice model" of juvenile corrections, which is based on the "just deserts" punishment philosophy, both correctional models amplify systemic deficiencies of school systems and completely disregard physiological development of adolescents and other bio-psycho-social factors that contribute to recidivism (Bartollas & Schmalleger, 2014, p. 309).

The crime control and justice models of juvenile corrections deemphasizes rehabilitative programming and are extensions of the human warehousing constructs of classical criminology. Specifically, the "rationality of crime" holds that all delinquent acts are rational choices made through a felicific calculus or risk-benefit analysis of the consequences for getting caught. This could not be further from the reality that juvenile crimes are wholly irrational and come from underdeveloped brains. Moreover, classical criminologists claim utilitarianism is the main principle of punishment-incarceration is a means to an end, not vengeful retaliation (Bartollas & Schmalleger, 2014, pp. 55–6). Like the disproven concept of deterrence via harsh sentences, utilitarian incarceration is belied by mass incarceration and high rates of recidivism. In other words, punishment-centric models contribute to crime and delinquency, which in turn exacerbates the school-to-prison-pipeline.

1

DYSFUNCTIONAL LEARNING

Why did I drop out of high school? Graduating should have been easy enough: attend class, listen, read, write, study, repeat. Ignore everything else. Do this and college becomes accessible, which can lead to a good paying job and a bright, fulfilling future. Avoid or screw up this process and the future becomes less stable and darker. Secondary school learning does not happen simply. Had I been mature, responsible, goal-oriented, and eager to learn, peer influence would have mattered less. My decisions would have been different. While I do not blame school for what happened, as an institution of learning they could have done more. No single relationship, event, or circumstance made me drop out; it was an avalanche of erroneous thinking, poor choices, and events that buried my ability to learn. Instead of a priority, high school became an impediment, and I lived without consideration of the consequences.

Entering high school was like jumping from a cliff: dark water waited underneath, frothing, and churning and drowning the unwary. Everyone takes the plunge with varying degrees of success and failure. I jumped without form or desire because going to school is an ordinary expectation of kids whether they understand its purpose or not.

My freshman year began with average grades and typical interests. I played the snare drum in the school marching band and joined the swim team, competing in various team and individual events. My classes ranked college preparatory (CP), a pre-selected path in public high school that readied students for SATs and application to most universities. Most students at Brunswick High attended CP classes.

There were two other class rankings: academically demanding advanced placement (AP), or general (G) classes, which often led to a GED and vocational courses rather than graduation. The CP path was chosen for me by a

DOI: 10.4324/9781003449454-2

junior high guidance counselor eager to please parents. Less so students. In a meeting with my parents he said, "Of course he's going to college, so CP classes are best. He can't focus enough for AP classes and G classes would be too easy for him."

Channeling students into pre-selected developmental paths, which could determine careers and earning potential, was not something I fully understood. To many students, it felt like segregation by socioeconomic status. AP students were often entitled, conceited, smug kids who generally got everything they wanted in and out of school. Their parents paid for tutors, took them to other countries over the summer, and acted as boosters or were members of the PTA. AP parents were so involved in school activities it often seemed like they ran the school, and their kids reaped the benefits.

AP classes held fewer students, giving teachers more one-on-one time for advanced lesson plans. Sometimes AP students, who were indeed intelligent, superior learners, attended CP classes because there was no advanced equivalent. Teachers in these classes called on AP students more, using their graded assignments and projects as examples to the rest of us. Rather than help, it generated resentment, annoyance, and jealousy, especially when teachers catered to AP students as a matter of course.

If CP students grew disgruntled by the blatant favoritism, G students, who also took CP classes when there was no lower equivalent, ignored or mocked the tension, but in some instances became genuinely discouraged. I felt bad for one girl who had dyslexia and struggled in English, nearing tears whenever we had reading assignments with essay responses. Many troublemakers attended G classes. They were often kids who came from broken homes and trailer park ghettos, wearing secondhand clothes and carrying books around by hand in shopping bags. They ate free lunch. School was a refuge, a place to escape a troubled home life. The AP, CP, and G distinctions were not indicative of success or failure, or a given family dynamic—it merely signaled a likely background, learning ability, and future.

Even knowing people learn at different rates did not lessen my annoyance with this high school caste system. It was ridiculous, and alongside the social pecking order typical of any high school, just another obstacle to getting an education. CP classes were not easy for me. High school in general required greater concentration and organization and I stayed disorganized-forgetting homework assignments, leaving books at school when I needed them for homework, rarely getting ahead of any classwork and giving a distracted half-effort in everything. It left me harried and overwhelmed and struggling to breathe.

Some days I went to class and paid attention, others were spent daydreaming about girls or nothing at all, never investing or listening. Fitting in mattered. The transition to high school marked a return to social obscurity, where the acknowledgement I received—even from teachers—was "Aren't you so-and-so's little brother?" Where before participation in the band, drama, football, and other sports—along with academic seniority—made junior high tolerable and occasionally fun, high school extracurriculars required tryouts. Being mediocre was not enough and freshmen were only selected if there were not enough upperclassmen to fill sports—like swimming.

Navigating new relationships, parental expectations, harder classes, the volatility of adolescence, and a new social hierarchy made life difficult. I began to hate school. Finding a place should not have consumed my thoughts or seemed impossible but it did not come naturally to me like it did for my peers. Junior high may have been a period of physical development, but high school quickly evolved into a full-blown adolescent identity crisis that challenged my Catholic upbringing and what my parents wanted. Everything I presumed to know took a back seat to the driving question: Who am I?

Nerd. Jock. Skater. Goth. Neo-hippy. "Grits" were a cross between blue collar tweekers and rednecks who dominated vocational classes and most likely owned a muscle car. "Preps" carried L.L. Bean backpacks and wore Adidas sneakers, flannel, and khaki pants. I was none of them. My family was middle-class, white, Catholic, my father college-educated and retired Navy, my mother college-educated and a stay-at-home piano teacher. Our lot was that of the average family in Brunswick. My older sister had been a "grit," my brother a neo-hippy. Interacting with every group in an attempt to belong, I felt like an outsider.

During freshman year, my mind wandered like a dog off the leash in a strange neighborhood. More distractions meant less attention to detail. No focus left me scattered and drifting from one class to the next, searching for something to anchor my thoughts to and feeling lost. Sometimes I absorbed things, but I began questioning the need. Why bother? Did other kids have the same problem? This fugue state disconnected from everything? Reaching out for help from a teacher, guidance counselor, or parent never crossed my mind because I barely understood the experience as a problem or precursor to something more. I also wanted to preserve my independence; asking for help would have been foolish to many teenagers, but for me it was tantamount to surrender on an unseen battlefield. Whatever I suffered would be done in silence.

Sampling different cliques and activities in an attempt to make friends extended to asking girls on dates, but these clumsy attempts either did not spark or fizzled like damp matches in the rain, merely reinforcing my awkwardness. Each experience failed to match this cloudy fantasy in my mind, one created from movies and TV shows, talk among friends since grade school, my parents' marriage, and the relationships of other couples. Despite the modeling, none of it served as good advice for an eager adolescent without a clue. I grew discouraged, withdrew, and found new outlets to alleviate stress, anxiety, and my poverty of thought.

I began using drugs and drinking alcohol without any serious intent beyond trying and liking being intoxicated. Despite an older sister who went to rehab for cocaine and alcohol addiction, and an uncle who was a long-time recovering alcoholic who talked of 12 Steps and going to AA meetings, I experimented with pot and alcohol with friends. I ultimately discovered in the euphoria of the high that nothing else mattered. But each high led to stealing as a way to pay for marijuana and alcohol. Both activities brought me into contact with other outcasts, kids who attended an alternative school for delinquents, kids who cared little about school and the rules. Their freedom fascinated me more than getting high and I wanted it. Consequences, long-term or short, were barely an afterthought. I lived in the moment.

At the time hanging around known delinquents, some of whom had been to the reformatory, did not seem like a bad idea. I saw them as streetwise kids who at least tolerated me enough to learn the secret of their independence. The cliché "birds of a feather flock together" was lost on me. Living beyond the governance of parents and teachers, coloring outside of the lines, appealed to some baser creature within me and it grew because I fed it. Parents and teachers began noticing the difference, however subtle, in my behavior, expressing concern over my lack of focus. I brushed them off, pretending everything was fine. Like every other teenager I wanted unadulterated freedom, not scrutiny and restrictions. Who my behavior impacted became less relevant than what I wanted, and by the end of freshman year my thoughts revolved around the next immediate pleasure, the next form of reckless entertainment that rejected plans, goals, structure, and the future.

A trio of upperclassmen had been allowing me to hang around and get high with them throughout the year. They introduced me to huffing aerosols, heavier drugs like cocaine and ketamine, and darker types of heavy metal music—the kind where the singer is screeching and impossible to understand, which was probably a good thing. Naivete and ignorance blinded me to the fact that these were some bad characters, but risky behavior does not account for character flaws, mine or theirs. It never occurred to me someone would take advantage of my desire to belong as a form of amusement.

My brother, a senior that year preparing for college, provided little guidance or insight beyond "Just stay cool and you'll do okay." What that meant was never explained. He was more concerned with his friends, having a good time, and moving out of the house. As his younger brother I represented inconvenience and being responsible for me was not a part of his plans. Normally, having a popular, respected older sibling attend the same school should have at least smoothed some of the problems I encountered, and it did enable conversations to a point. But I did not want to be identified as so-and-so's little brother and, however cool they may have been, my brother's neo-hippy friends were not my friends.

The irony of high school is this belief adolescents, despite having an underdeveloped prefrontal cortex where decision making occurs, make good decisions like adults. It is as if upon entering high school maturity, responsibility, and future orientation become norms instead of developmental mile markers with blurred lines. Just as everyone does not learn at the same rate, everyone does not develop at the same rate. My underdeveloped decision making extended everywhere but was most apparent in my choice of companions.

The trio of upperclassmen I had been hanging around had a bad reputation among the student body, mainly because they were outcasts who mocked others with an insouciance that fascinated me. It was as if they had a special power that cut through social hierarchy. Though they initially accepted me, they took my need for role models as something to be exploited. Over time their mocking was turned on me and evolved into threats and an ultimatum: bring us money or else.

Out of fear over what might happen, and acknowledgement little could be accomplished on my own, I asked my brother for help. It seemed reasonable to believe he would prevent me from getting beaten up, but I was mistaken. My brother thought giving me money to pay off a trio of bullies would be easier than getting involved. Maybe he felt it was my problem to deal with and this expiated anything he refused to do. Maybe he thought I deserved it. Whatever his reasons, my brother gave me a twenty-dollar bill after promising to help and left me to handle the trio of upperclassmen on my own.

Rather than give in I tucked away the money and went to the red brick building, a place where some students smoked before and after school. Intent on ending the threats and standing up for myself, I tried fighting one of the trio and failed, falling to the ground and getting pummeled. In the end it was not the beating that hurt so much as my brother watching it from the sideline as if he did not know me.

That day I learned the wrong lesson behind the red brick building. Rather than change my behavior or the people I spent time with, the beating and humiliation were indicators I needed to toughen up. Destroying my weakness and inexperience meant becoming more reckless and self-destructive and independent of everyone. Combined with poor self-esteem and complete disregard for normal behavior, I began self-mutilating, burning my arms with cigarettes as a way to show the bullies who publicly humiliated me that I did not fear pain. I saw it as a statement: they could not hurt me as much as I could hurt myself and if I willingly did this to myself where does that leave them? The results were mixed. The trio of upperclassmen backed off, but so did the few friends I had. My parents found out about the burns and demanded answers, but after some gymnastic-like lying (an accident with bacon grease rather than intentional burns) they left me alone.

The beginning of my sophomore year should not have focused on arriving at the red brick building with a newly formed self-destructive attitude. The unexpected benefit of my heedlessness was a release from anxiety, fear of failure, concern over others' expectations of me, or much of anything else that previously wounded my spirit. I stopped caring. About everything.

School became a place I went to get high, check out girls, or go on excursions to steal alcohol and cigarettes. One of the major signs of what was to come happened one morning before school. I sat in the back of a van smoking pot and huffing aerosols. We were parked across the street from the school's front entrance, music machine-gunning from the speakers. I stumbled out of the van, struggling to focus and realizing I missed homeroom and first period biology. In that moment I stopped being a tardy student and fully assumed the new identity of a mentally ill juvenile delinquent making incredibly stupid, short-sighted, self-destructive decisions. I glanced at the blurred edifice of high school, gave it the middle finger, and got back in the van. A few days later I dropped out and ran away from home.

2

INSTITUTIONAL LEARNING

After running away from home and committing a string of petty thefts, I was court-ordered to Maine Youth Center (MYC) pending a hearing. Juveniles at the state's oldest reformatory were typically assigned credits to be reduced by working in the laundry or kitchen, receiving good conduct reports and going to school. Though this took time, a diligent resident could complete a 90-credit charge in 30 days. Except immaturity often got in my way, most kids had multiple charges, and probation officers or case workers usually had the final say. For juveniles, leaving MYC was difficult.

About 35 hold-for-courts like me were assigned to Cottage One. We had no contact with residents from other cottages, our undetermined status a potential liability and threat to institutional security. Regardless of the isolation, all of us hoped for an alternative to credits or commitment (drug rehab, probation, or a group home) because anything was better than time at MYC. Anything.

As wards of the state charged or convicted of various crimes we became "less than," castoffs even some family barely gave a second thought. Kids under 18 in the free world do not enjoy the same respect as adults, but once they enter the criminal justice system reasonable care, rights, and human dignity are traded for enmity. MYC staff took our incarceration as a license to treat us in any way they saw fit; those who disagree with it largely kept silent, not working to make waves or lose their jobs.

Aside from fear and intimidation, MYC rules were military-strict and backed by the certainty of consequences like solitary confinement, extra work, or a written "plan." Staff punished without leniency, and plans were their favorite. This single page essay was a consequence for infractions like talking during a silent period, getting up without permission, back talking,

DOI: 10.4324/9781003449454-3

antagonizing, or any whim that seized a given staff member. Plans explained "what you did, why you did it, and what you'll do to avoid it next time," and took as long as it took to write. Some kids hated writing plans so much they chose going to the hole, but this rarely worked because the plan awaited their return.

Free conversation was a luxury at MYC, a reward extended when staff felt benevolent. Otherwise, silence dominated day and night, hunting misbehavior, and mauling those brave enough to speak or laugh aloud without permission. Want to use the toilet? Hand in the air and wait to be recognized. Have an emergency? Hand in the air. Sharpen a pencil? Hand. Get up in the middle of the night to vomit? Hand. Move without permission—plan. Move aggressively or argue—solitary confinement. When I was asked to attend school, I responded without thinking and said, "Yes! Please!" while getting up from the table. This earned a scowl from the staff who posed the question. And a plan.

School in Cottage one consisted of educational games and GED testing. I was ineligible for the GED exam during my first MYC stint (state law required anyone under eighteen to have been out of school for a year and unable to return), so the teacher—Ms. Preyl—administered a pre-test to measure my ability. I tried hard, mainly to prove that while I made bad decisions and was disenchanted with learning, this didn't make me stupid. The problem was that between my Catholic upbringing and nagging conscience lay this belief my actions held no long-term implications. I was so immersed in the present it blinded me to the future as if it would never exist. Passing the GED pre-test should have alerted me to my potential as a student, but I dismissed it as little more than a way to pass the time.

Within a month the court ordered me to attend a long-term drug rehab, my release from MYC dependent upon completion of the program. Project Rebound was intended to last six months. While there, residents attended AA and NA meetings with six other juvenile residents, some of whom also agreed to rehab as an alternative to MYC. We listened to grizzled winos and skeletal crackheads talk of sleeping on the street, hustling family members, and squandering their lives. I struggled to identify with them. Their experiences were nothing like mine, which were relatively innocuous and experimental. I lived in a small coastal town where any drugs were hard to find and buying alcohol required the help of a wiling wino. I had never been employed beyond a paper route and did not even have a license or car. In no way did I consider myself an alcoholic or addict. Project Rebound was an escape from MYC and the threats it represented, nothing else.

Between counseling sessions and meetings, I attended more GED prep classes and began to understand why my junior high guidance counselor steered me away from G level classes. They're simple. Our teachers encouraged us to try, keeping the topics interesting, but not expecting much since they knew most of us would quit the program or be returned to the reformatory. It helped these teachers, like Ms. Preyl, cared enough to try, shared attention equally, and made personal connections so that school became a welcome relief from institutional life.

My problems went deeper than a lack of discipline and interest in school. Immature, struggling to develop an identity, lacking a mentor or role model, drugs might have been a potential problem, but they ranked well below self-esteem and anxiety issues. I did not belong in rehab. Accepting such a thing meant admitting a weakness and fallibility I did not feel. It meant acknowledging my substance use was more than a good time with friends, that it was self-destructive behavior. Believing I knew myself better than any adult makes changing my behavior or considering my mental health impossible. Personal awareness that inventoried all my faults, responsibility, submission, and atonement were foreign concepts and the more it was forced on me the more resisted.

All I wanted was the freedom to make mistakes without being shoved into one institution or another. Why did *my* life require order and constraint? Why wasn't I free to explore the world and make mistakes? Sure, my "mistakes" put me on probation, and every mundane error in judgment after that could be punished with incarceration. But if I learned anything from my first foray into the criminal justice system, mistakes, even by juveniles, are never treated lightly or as if they happen by accident.

I was kicked out of Project Rebound for allegedly threatening a staff member. My protests against this accusation were ignored. No juvenile on loan from MYC would get the benefit of any doubt. A counselor called Bangor PD and by nightfall they returned me to the reformatory.

On the way to MYC as dread made it harder to breathe, I wondered how institutional "discipline" would lead to my adult-like behavior. All that I had been shown is those with the authority did whatever they wanted to people without it. Many of the adults at MYC and Project Rebound punished arbitrarily and excessively and did not care how their "lessons" impacted us as long as we obeyed. Verbal and physical abuse under the guise of corrections demanded attention like a lash but engendered hatred and distrust for authority. They punished domestic disputes between parents and their kids. Punished learning disabilities. And punished mental illness. As if we had choices in these things. It taught all of us that, if we could not help ourselves, why should anyone else?

A few days after returning to MYC I stole a razor from a staff member's desk and cut myself. Staff soon discovered the theft and my freshly cut arms, and immediately put me in the intensive control unit (ICU), MYC's version of solitary confinement.

Fear lanced self-injurious thoughts like an ugly boil when they told me to strip naked, gave me a tear—resistant blanket and thin mattress, and put me into a cell. A window covered in rusted steel mesh lit the 6ft x 8ft space in grey shadows. A yellow light in the ceiling made it seem darker, as if its florescence revealed truths too vile for normal light. Nothing to read. No radio or television. Reduced meals. No way to tell time.

ICU was a wing of ten attached to the infirmary building. Where libraries muted noise and silent periods were frequently interrupted, ICU entombed sound and hope together. We offset this by whispering through a crack at the bottom of our cell doors: stories about home, music, girls, how long we had at MYC, and why we were in ICU. Threading these conversations was a need for companionship and the ardent belief that this could abate our fears for a while.

When the outer hallway door buzzed open all whispering stopped. No need to give staff an excuse to open one of our cells, or, or put us in restraints (usually zip ties or handcuffs by the ankles and wrists together). Bobby, a sandy-haired 14-year-old from Aroostook County, decided he had enough of ICU staff. He swore at them, kicked his door and slung food beneath it, and otherwise refused to calm down because they shorted him a lunch tray (for a prior complaint about small portions). When they came, there were four carrying mace, zip ties, and handcuffs. None of us could see it but we didn't need to. Bobby screamed. Flesh smacked flesh and a thud vibrated the floor.

"We told you to shut the fuck up Bobby, now look what you made us do."
Bobby cried out.

A quick succession of thuds and grunts echoed in the hallway. Bobby crying and pleading. Two ICU staff came out of the cell laughing. Three or four meaty thumps, like the sound of a kicked pumpkin, then the remaining staff slammed the cell door shut and left Bobby moaning and crying.

No one questioned or stopped the beatings, withheld meals, denied showers, and the rest because ICU staff dealt with MYC "problems" as they saw fit. They were aggressive, vicious, cruel, and notorious for their violence; their reputation often enough to calm troublemakers.

Time passed. Maybe a week. Maybe two. Filthy gray light creeping through the window and meals marked the time. I thought of my family. I thought of my classmates and wondered what they were reading in *Ancient Medieval History*, wishing I had a book or something. When panic pushed a scream against my teeth, I prised a sharp stone from the floor and dragged it across my arms, quietly sang half-remembered songs, or tapped my head against the wall until a headache overcame other thoughts. Prayer didn't initially come to mind, but a few days after Bobby's beating, I was on my knees begging "Takemeaway. Godtakemeaway. Godpleasetakemeaway." It was both a chant and plea muttered until the fear passed or sleep came. Or the outer door to the hallway buzzed open.

By the time they returned me to Cottage One, I saw with different eyes. On the surface I kept silent and did whatever was expected of me, pretending solitary confinement had been a character-building experience. Underneath my blood seethed with the need to run forever and never look back, to escape MYC and its hellish overseers, to escape the buried silence and filthy gray light of ICU. What I could not have known or anticipated is how much this experience hardened me, and made me care even less about the future, or myself.

Several weeks later, my probation officer asked if I wanted to go home. He knew about MYC; he heard the stories from other kids and seemed genuinely reluctant to commit me.

"I know you want to go home. You're not like a lot of these guys. You're not a hard ass. You have a family that loves and wants you home."

My parents, supportive and forgiving, were willing to take me back. The incident at Project Rebound would be overlooked since no charges were filed, but the conditions for my return home would be strict. Obey curfew, attend school or work, and meet my PO every other week. If I ran away or violated the conditions, it was back to the youth center. I agreed, would have agreed to anything, to get away from MYC.

When I got home, Mom met with the superintendent of Brunswick schools to re-enroll me only to discover I had been expelled from the system. Not even the pre-delinquent alternative school, where kids worked through G level courses in a smaller class, would accept me. All of them had greater delinquent experiences than my own, which was annoying in many ways. The apparent difference is that I pled guilty to breaking and entering a number of cars, unauthorized use of a motor vehicle, and vandalism. The plea deal for probation and drug rehab had cost enrollment in the Brunswick school system. My annoyance was short-lived; I didn't really want to be back in school.

Mom tried to help me. Private school or connecting to another town were not options—too expensive—so she decided to teach me at home. This occurred before online schools or affordable PCs—Windows 2.0 and the Macintosh, a big, boxy PC with a slot in the front for a hard disk, were relatively new in 1995 and not as ubiquitous as tech would become in school. With a library card and electric IBM typewriter, mom attempted to keep me interested in learning, but her effort fizzled when I put nothing into it. Later, she enrolled me in an adult night class on writing in Thopsham, the town across the river, while I looked for jobs during the day. Both felt like an effort to delay the inevitable.

I got a job at McDonald's cooking and cleaning, grateful to be doing something productive and out of the house. The stability of a job and paycheck boosted my self-esteem in ways school had not. I enjoyed the work, which was simple, and people, liking how for eight hours a day I could be competent and needed. For the first time I had money to spend and considered saving for a car. My parents discussed getting my driver's permit and earning a GED, maybe even enlisting in the military. I listened and nodded, interested but not invested. Working felt like enough and I had no ambition or direction beyond that.

After three months of work and obeying the conditions of my probation I was allowed the freedom to go over to a friend's house. This quickly became the excuse I used to smoke pot or hang out downtown with kids who had been to MYC or had dropped out of school to work. On the way home from one such occasion I was dared to steal a mirror from a delivery truck in a parking lot. In the moment it seemed a minor thing, made funny by the influence of marijuana. A worker in a donut shop saw me, ran out of the store, and wrestled me to the ground. A bystander called the police. My "friends" disappeared. When Brunswick's PD showed up the arresting officer recognized me and called my PO, who sent me back to MYC.

Upon returning to Cottage One I affected an air of injustice. No crime had been committed (had the donut shop employee not stopped me I would have taken the mirror) and it seemed like an overreaction to lock me up again. Staff greeted me like a regular, which should have bothered me but didn't, and offered me a job with the kitchen crew. I accepted knowing the work would break up a monotonous day and provide extra food. It was better than reading battered copies of *National Geographic* and sitting in silence.

Time moved so slowly that days and nights stuttered across the horizon. I began preparing for the GED exam, having been out of school for a year. There were six of us in the GED prep class, one of the guys I met at Project Rebound, another in ICU. Ms. Preyl and Ms. Leath made learning fun by providing small rewards for correct answers and our attention. The exam covered everything a public high school sophomore should know. Ms. Preyl mentioned college as a possibility in the future, but most of us scoffed at the idea since it required more schooling and money our families did not have. Scholarships were never mentioned, nor was there any discussion about why college would be needed or how we would go about enrolling. The MYC teachers could not sell us on a fantasy. College was unimaginable and disconnected from our current problems. Ms. Leath simply smiled and gave her usual reply to our cynicism.

"You'll never know until you try."

MYC school was a relief because it created a sense of urgency to the process, as if at any moment the right to an education would be snatched away or trampled upon by staff who thought we all belonged in a hole. Maybe this pressure was an advantage, and when combined with a place devoid of distractions, would lead to academic success. I had no way of knowing. School in the youth center meant freedom. School in the free world meant problems. At MYC we recognized our effort was inextricably linked to the value of our independence. Give a half-assed effort and it seems you don't want to go home; maybe if I knew giving a half-assed effort in high school would lead to MYC and a cycle of confinement, I would have tried harder. Aligning educational success on the inside worked, but the same could not be said of earning a GED and succeeding in the free world. A GED did not teach me any important life skills that made incarceration less likely—it was a simply a check in an institutional box that opened the front gate.

3

CLASS DISMISSED

Head resting against the cold steel cell door, I listened as a kid in the hall talked about his mother prostituting herself for heroin and leaving her children to fend for themselves. It made me feel out of place—my mom worked and taught piano and still made sure we brushed our teeth and got to school. My parents had a loving relationship and dad worked a white-collar job. Both went to college. The disembodied voice of a 15-year-old drifted under the door. He got arrested for stealing a bike. Because he ran from the cops when they caught and brought him to MYC, they put him in ICU. Juveniles who ran from law enforcement in Maine were automatically put in solitary confinement at the youth center. I found out the hard way.

Hanging out in front of Amato's Pizza, high, I had violated my probation and knew the Police were looking for me. I went over to a friend's house the day before to smoke pot with a girl who seemed to like me and missed my curfew. Going home late and high was not an option: my parents would call my PO, who would violate me anyway. So, I stayed gone and continued getting high. Sitting on Main Street as if the cops would not find me was an act of defiance.

A police cruiser pulled into the parking lot. I got up and walked away.

"Lyle May!"

Out of the corner of my eye I saw a cop on his radio, fast walking toward me.

"Lyle May! Stop!"

I ran, cutting across rush hour traffic, dodging between cars amidst the blare of horns. Too high to be afraid, run fast, or realize running was a bad idea. I made it to an open parking lot with thoughts of a nearby river, then the cop caught up and tackled me. My run barely lasted two minutes.

DOI: 10.4324/9781003449454-4

At MYC they processed and brought me to the ICU wing. Unlike the first time, they told me it would be for a minimum of two weeks, my penalty for running. If I acted up, the time would be extended two days. The door slammed shut behind me, a familiar fear scraped fingers down my spine. Looking at the yellowed-white walls and dim lighting, it was as if I never really left, or had taken a brief vacation to freedom.

Sleep never came that night. I wondered how getting high and not going home could really be crimes. Being punished for such little things seemed ridiculous when many of my delinquent peers did much worse. Telling me this was prevention—as my PO did—or that my parents believed it necessary— they did not but had had no other answers—failed to make the time easy or justifiable in my mind. Staring at the rusted metal mesh on the cell window, it was difficult to believe anyone cared.

Before returning to Cottage One, I discovered the other penalty for runners: shackles and a bright orange jumpsuit. MYC had no fences, only an AWOL squad with the authority to chase runners anywhere they went. As ruthless as some bounty hunters, the AWOL squad took preventative measures. Anywhere on MYC property I would be in shackles and the easily visible jumpsuit. Since I already had a GED and would not be allowed to work since I was a designated "runner," my time at MYC would stretch.

After a month, my PO came to visit. When I shuffled in, shackles clicking, he frowned. He had warned me against becoming a "recidivist" though he never really explained beyond saying, "Somebody who's going to live in prison and visit the free world if he doesn't get his shit together." It was my fourth stay at MYC.

Face blank, he said, "I guess you're ready to go home?"

I started to speak, but he raised a hand to stop me.

"Your parents don't want you to come home, Lyle."

"What?" Shock. Hurt.

"They're worried you'll come home high. Rob them blind or put yourself in danger." He looked at me.

My eyes stung. "I would never do that!" Cold sweat trickled down my back. "I was just smoking pot! Not shooting or snorting anything. My brother ..."

"Your brother isn't in shackles. Marijuana is illegal and you are on probation."

"But they can't be serious!" My voice cracked.

"They are. So am I. You should be committed. You're not learning anything."

I begged him not to commit me to the Maine Youth Center, which could be until my twenty-first birthday. I pled for another chance, hoping he would grant it, but not expecting much.

After a long two weeks my PO agreed to admit me into Day One, a long-term drug rehab. First, though, he released me to a group home as a test, and to await bed space at Day One. Despite the initial surprise over my parents' refusal to let me come home, I was not really angry. Their concerns were easy enough to understand. All of it, however, was lost in the relief I would soon leave MYC.

During this period of my life, I was a teenager reacting to situations without any strategy or goal in mind. Thinking, if it ever occurred, came after the fact when it was too late to consider consequences. The future, both vague and unknowable, became a place with little hindsight and no foresight. As a result, I struggled to connect my misfortune with my bad habits and mental failures. Rehab never struck me as a place to learn about making better choices: it was an escape. In my mind it is all that mattered.

The group homes consisted of half–a-dozen boys between 13 and 17 living in a converted split-level ranch. Some were transitioning to other programs, like Job Corps or rehab, to avoid MYC. A few boys lived there because they had nowhere else to go. The youngest, an underfed brown-headed kid named Perry, asked about my family. I gave him the answer that made sense, devoid of sarcasm or affected toughness: "I wore out my welcome."

In the shadow of MYC, having just been cut some slack for what was likely the last time, the thought of running never really crossed my mind. Between the fresh fear of incarceration and clarity of sobriety I only wanted to smoke a cigarette, and not stand in line naked, waiting for a two-minute shower while staff watched and shouted to hurry up. I hated lines, being counted, itemized, and treated like property. I hated being under the threat of violence if I forgot to ask permission to use the toilet or even looked defiant. These things embodied MYC, were justified by the law, endorsed by the public, and influenced the life of every kid in the institution.

It should have been no surprise I made fucked-up decisions.

Day One was located on a hill in a tall, two-story house with a wing of rooms added to one side for male residents, administrative offices and a lobby for visitors. Female residents lived on the top floor of the house. This surprised me. MYC held female juvenile offenders but were separated from the rest of us, with few exceptions and intense scrutiny. Day One was very different.

At full capacity, the rehab held ten residents and was not as dysfunctional as Project Rebound or lax like the group home. There were assigned chores, counseling sessions, group activities, meal planning, school, and structured "free time." At the heart of its operation, Day One required residents to be honest, rigorous, and responsible in applying the 12 Steps of Alcoholics Anonymous to their recovery. Maturity and self-control were also emphasized.

Transitioning out of Day One included getting a job, apartment, placement at a community college, and creation of a one-year-plan on how to maintain success through sobriety. Reaching this point was expected to take a year or more of hard work, but those who graduated from the program became capable adults, living a clean life in the free world.

I never thought of myself as capable or successful. When the director of Day One outlined these goals, I nodded as if it all made perfect sense, but in my mind, it sounded like beachfront property in Arizona: ridiculously unattainable.

Day One had no locked doors. Residents stayed voluntarily. I could leave at any time, but doing so would violate my probation, of which eight months remained. Plenty of time to screw up and get committed to MYC for three years. I was still on loan from the State.

The teachers at Day One did not care about GEDs. They put me to work on high school level, college preparatory material, giving me the goals of graduation from high school with a diploma, adequate preparation for the SAT, and enrollment in college courses. The excuses of addiction, learning disabilities, thwarted desires, and mental illness were not tolerated—as if such things could be willed away and overcome by mental toughness. It worked for a little while.

I cannot say with any surety that if Day One had been a male-only rehab I would have successfully graduated the program. Finding and falling in love, engaging in a sexually-active relationship, considering marriage with my girlfriend while we both lived under the same threat of re-incarceration, and planning a semblance of a future together were the last things I expected to experience. I went to Day One with the intent of doing the right things, but it did not work out that way. I won't apologize for loving someone.

Of course, this did not make me any less impulsive or reckless. For nearly three months we engaged in unprotected sex, midnight rendezvous, and stolen moments until another resident caught on and told on us. The most responsible thing either of us did was to come clean during a group, something constantly stressed by counselors if we broke rules. Sexual relationships were forbidden, so rather than wait to be kicked out we called our POs and asked permission to leave the program.

By then I had turned 18, which seemed like a small miracle itself, and this likely played a role in what happened next. Both my PO and parents were glad I finally made an adult decision by calling and asking instead of running off. My parents would allow me to come home if I stayed clean, worked, and looked for another place.

So, I went home and obeyed the rules. A few weeks after my probation ended in May 1996, I moved into the living room of a friend's apartment. It was a mistake.

No longer under the threat of the Maine Youth Center I celebrated by drinking, smoking pot, and dropping LSD. My long-distance romance evaporated, as did my savings. After losing my job, I bounced checks from my empty savings account. When those ran out and the police came looking for me about some stolen cars (of which I had no knowledge), I simply left.

An open road of opportunity and unadulterated freedom stretched before me. On it I hitch-hiked to Vermont, partied until I couldn't remember my name, went to some Grateful Dead shows and tried to bury my adolescence as if it happened to someone else. I tried to forget and move on, but it did not last.

At the end of the summer, I went home, ultimately squashing the issue of any stolen cars (someone used my name to throw the police off their trail). I worked out a deal with a Brunswick detective to avoid larceny charges for bounced checks, getting two jobs to pay off the debt and living with my parents while doing so.

I absorbed little from rehab, though understanding why is not hard. I was an irresponsible teenager who though he knew what was best. After being bounced in and out MYC, rehab, and the group home, this lack of stability made my impulsive, self-destructive tendencies worse. I pursued freedom like a drug and never quite understood how it intertwined with independence and self-sufficiency. I had no skills or plans for a responsible adult life, or ever had a mentor to guide me there. Clueless, stubborn, beaten by my choices and experiences as a ward of the State, I was bound to fail.

While working two jobs to pay off my debt, money for pot came from shoplifting excursions. When there was none to be had I huffed aerosols or anything that had fumes. I contemplated suicide, flirting with the final escape it would provide, but never fully committed to its embrace. I knew I needed help. Not rehab or incarceration but hospitalization. There was more to my problem than bad places, addiction, and a lack of education.

The final straw for my parents came when I was caught trying to take one of my dad's checks. They promptly kicked me out.

I left Maine with the vague idea of visiting family down south, catching a bus to Virginia Beach then living near Richmond before a similar dysfunctional pattern developed; work, get high, lose job, wear out my welcome, and leave with the vain hope something better awaited in another town or state.

That I was mentally ill is not something I would admit to. Self-analysis is not something I knew how to do. My worst self-destructive compulsions manifested, not under the influence of any substance, but in the shadows of its valleys where all my mistakes awaited acknowledgement. Ever defiant, by the time I arrived in Asheville, North Carolina, in January of 1997, I was running from the past and myself and couldn't get away fast enough.

Sometimes I think about what it would have been like to finish school and to walk on stage in a cap and gown to receive a diploma with my peers. It's a short-lived image. My sophomore, junior and senior years were squandered getting high in the streets and suffering the consequences in institutions. In places reserved for people who cannot "get their shit together," I learned that, if you are unable to help yourself, fail to follow the rules, or are oblivious to how these "choices" matter, falling through the cracks of society is easy. Once that happens, it is a long way to the bottom.

References

Akers, R. L., Sellers, C. S., & Jennings, W. G. (2017). *Criminological theories: Introduction, Evaluation, and Application.* Oxford University Press.

Bartollas, C., & Schmalleger, F. (2014). *Juvenile Delinquency* (9th ed.). Pearson.

Campaign for Youth Justice (2012). Key facts: Youth in the justice system. Retrieved from: www.campaignforyouthjustice.org/images/factsheets/KeyYouthCrimeFactsJune72016final.pdf.

Cohen, A. K. (1955). *Delinquent Boys: The Future of the Gang.* Free Press.

Hagan, J. (1991). Destiny and drift: Subcultural preferences, status attainments, and the risk and rewards of youth. *American Sociological Review*, 56(5), 567–582.

Hirschi, T. (1969). *Causes of Delinquency.* University of California Press.

Kandel, D., & Yamaguchi, K. (1993). From beer to crack: Developmental patterns of drug involvement. *American Journal of Public Health*, 83(6), 851–855.

McClelland, G. M., Teplin, L. A., & Abram, K. M. (2004). Detention and prevalence of substance use among juvenile detainees. Office of Juvenile Justice and Delinquency. www.ojp.gov/pdffiles1/ojjdp/203934.pdf.

Mover, M., & Nelis, A. (2018). *The Meaning of Life: The Case for Abolishing Life Sentences.* The New Press.

Payne, A. A., & Welch, K. (2010). Modeling the effects of racial threat on punitive and restorative school discipline. *Criminology*, 48(4), 1019–1062. doi:10.1111/j.17459125.2010.00211.x.

Pesta, R. (2018). Labeling and the differential impact of school discipline on negative life outcomes: Assessing ethno-racial variation in the school-to-prison pipeline. *Crime and Delinquency*, 64(11), 1489–1512.

Sutherland, E. H. (1956). A statement of the theory. In A. Cohen, A. Lindesmith, & K. Schuessler (Eds), *The Sutherland Papers* (pp. 7–29). Indiana University Press.

PART 2

Moral Panic: Abandoning the Rehabilitative Ideal

According to the Federal Bureau of Investigations (FBI), the violent crime rate per 100,000 people rose from less than 200 to over 700 in the period between 1960 and 1995 (Baumgartner et al., 2021). This "crime wave" could have been contextualized with normal population growth, urbanization, economic downturns, and the fight for civil rights amongst the marginalized. Instead, "public" concern was focused on the federal government's "War on Drugs" and "War on Crime." As a result, by the early 1990s, the white middle-class attitude toward crime echoed the populist sentiment of "taking back the streets" from "thugs" and "hoodlums." Following a series of laws pursued by conservative lawmakers, being tough on crime translated into an expanded criminal legal system, draconian punishments, and the highest imprisonment rate per capita in the world. In 1970, there were 196,441 people in prison; by 2000, the prison population exploded to 1,394,231 (The World Almanac Book of Facts, 2020). By year-end in 2019, the Bureau of Justice Statistics reported state and federal prison populations at over 1,430,000.

The moral panic around crime led to a shift in penal philosophy. Policymakers abandoned the rehabilitative ideal and racialized criminal behavior in response to the civil rights era, primarily targeting the urban poor with aggressive policing. Some of the punitive fervor came from criminologist Robert Martinson's "What works? Questions and answers about prison reform." After a review of over 200 studies of correctional rehabilitation programs, Martinson's article provided the summary that, with few exceptions, rehabilitative programs have "no appreciable effect on recidivism" (Martinson, 1974, p. 25). In 1974, Martinson appeared on 60 Minutes and reiterated the idea that "nothing works" to rehabilitate prisoners. Political pundits, lawmakers across the political spectrum, federal judges, and some corrections

DOI: 10.4324/9781003449454-5

leaders took Martinson's claim, along with rising crime rates and social upheaval, to pursue congressional change (Goodman et al., 2017). That congressional change manifested in the 1984 Sentencing Reform Act, which lengthened federal prison sentences, eliminated parole, implemented life without parole for many crimes, and invoked Martinson and others to justify the policy changes (Goodman et al., 2017).

The U.S. Supreme Court upheld the more punitive sentencing guidelines of the 1984 Sentencing Reform Act in Mistretta v. United States (1989). The Court cited a 1983 Senate report, the same one that relied on Martinson's (1974) article, as though it was drawn from a broad swath of criminological research, not one criminologist's research: "The report referred to the 'outmoded rehabilitation model' for federal criminal sentencing and recognized that the efforts of the criminal justice system to achieve rehabilitation of offenders had failed" (*Mistretta v. United States*, 1989, footnote 3).

Law enforcement militarized, and framed police work in urban communities as entering a "combat zone." Naturally, the people were treated as enemy combatants. Schools were prisonized, amplifying institutional failures with an increased use of exclusionary discipline. The complicated, centuries-long debate over how to address youth crime was neatly packaged with the label "super-predators" (Baumgartner et al., 2021).

Like Martinson (1974), academic John J. Di Iulio provided an article that channeled fears of the white middle-class majority, presenting urban street crime as a threat to American values and public safety. "The coming of the super-predator" (Di Iulio, 1995) dehumanized minority youth with patently racist rhetoric. Most damaging of all was the false prediction that unless something was done immediately, youth crime would increase exponentially as gangs from "black inner-city neighborhoods" committed "homicidal violence, in 'wolf packs' ... often murdering their victims in groups of two or more" (as cited in Baumgartner, et al. 2021).

Many professionals in the criminal legal and penal fields argued against the "never-ending punishments," emphasizing how these "super-predators" were adolescents who would age out of crime and change in a rehabilitative environment (Baumgartner et al. 2021). Penal experts pointed out the crippling costs of mass incarceration and dangers of long-term confinement without incentives for good behavior or meaningful educational programs. As Baumgartner, et al. (2021) writes: "Dissenting voices screamed at in the professional journals, but to no avail" (p. 6). It was too late—Martinson (1974), Di Iulio (1995), and sensationalized depictions of crime in the media had created a moral panic.

Goode and Ben-Yehuda (2009) assert that moral panics are "characterized by the feeling ... evildoers pose a threat to society and to the moral order as a consequence of their behavior ... something must be done about it, and that something must be done now" (as cited in Kappeler & Potter, 2018, p. 36).

That "something" became the 1994 Violent Crime Control and Law Enforcement Act (VCCLEA), also known as the 1994 Omnibus Crime Bill.

The prison industrial complex boomed. States earned billions of dollars in federal funding if they toughened sentencing policy and eliminated parole, implemented mandatory minimums, and increased use of LWOP. Attached to the 1994 Omnibus Crime Bill, but not originally part of the VCCLEA, was a measure that eliminated access to Pell Grants for the incarcerated. Amidst the proliferation of life sentences nothing epitomized the end of fact-based corrections more than the end of college-in-prison programs.

Incarcerated people had been enrolling in college correspondence courses since the 1920s, but post-secondary education (PSCE) programs were not offered in U.S. prisons until the mid-1970s (Page, 2004). The increase in PSCE programs is attributed to the Title IV of the 196 Higher Education Act, which instituted the Basic Educational Opportunity Grant Program-named the Pell Grant in 1980 after Senator Claiborne Pell [D-RI] (Page, 2004). The Pell Grant program provided federal funding for low and middle-income students who could not have afforded college on their own. Pell Grants became the primary source of funding for PSCE programs because nearly everyone in prison lacks an income and most state legislatures refused to fund higher education for prisoners (Lawrence, 1994).

The rise of the tough-on-crime era made public officials uncomfortable using taxpayer money for PSCE programs, or advocating for the incarcerated in any way, even if it made sense. After the 1994 Omnibus Crime Bill came the 1995 Prison Litigation Reform Act (PLRA), which restricted an incarcerated person's access to the courts when filing civil complaints about conditions of confinement. Next, Congress passed the 1996 Anti-terrorism and Effective Death Penalty Act (AEDPA), which was intended to speed up executions, but instead gutted the federal *habeus corpus* petition and prisoners' access to the federal courts, The VCCLEA, PLRA, and AEDPA signaled a new penal philosophy: human warehousing (Feely & Simon, 1992 as cited in Page, 2004).

What one does in prison, and what is done to them, matters. Eliminating PSCE programs made it less likely prisoners could return to the community as productive members of society because, in addition to all the collateral consequences of a felony record and insufficient skills for economic mobility, society sent the clear message that incarcerated people are worthless. Without essential learning and qualifications for salaried employment in an increasingly technological world, no critical thinking or organizational skills, and only some vocational training while in prison, those who did get out struggled (Page, 2004). People return to prison, in part, because programming is deficient—when it should teach resilience, critical thinking skills, and provide marketable credentials in the form of a college degree, instead the incarcerated are taught menial labor.

Prison populists believe menial labor—food service, janitorial work, construction, and other physical labor that requires no education or credential—is all the incarcerated need to learn because the new American underclass should be comprised of laborers, not thinkers. Anything more coddled criminals and threatened the middle-class. Adherence to a "just deserts" approach to incarceration entrenched classism and racism into a criminal legal system some academics claim is the new slavery (Alexander, 2010). By ignoring how poverty remains tied to some element of the criminal legal system and never have a realistic pathway to the American dream.

According to some lawmakers, the privilege of a college degree means the exclusion of anyone who breaks the law. Representative Bart Gordon [D-TN], a primary sponsor of the Congressional measure that ended Pell Grant access in prison, argued that the privilege of college is wasted on the incarcerated. Ultimately, rehabilitation in prison is an anomaly amongst swine:

> Just because one blind hog may occasionally find an acorn does not mean other blind hogs will. The same principle applies to giving Federal Pell Grants to prisoners. Certainly, there is an occasional success story, but when virtually every prisoner in America is eligible ... taxpayers lose.
>
> *(Page, 2004, p. 364)*

In a 1994 letter to James Clyburn (D-SC), corrections officials and top penal experts around the country explained that PSCE programs helped maintain carceral order, improve the institutional climate, and allow prisoners to develop pro-social, non-criminal, non-violent identities (Page, 2004). It was a rare occasion when penal experts and corrections officials advocated for something the incarcerated badly needed and wanted. Many corrections officials and wardens knew a future without PSCE programs would lead to the violent decay of prisons and ultimately risk public safety. Reason and experience fell to the fever of retributive justice and populism, which had always contained a rotten core of anti-intellectualism, the antithesis of higher learning.

The school-to-prison pipeline (STPP) is a distinctly social construction, a collection of flawed disciplinary policies that target BIPOC community and mentally ill youth and push them out of school where justice system involvement becomes more likely. As such, misinformation disseminated by conservative and populist lawmakers in turn influences harsher laws that feed the carceral state with disadvantaged youth. In prison, the disadvantage is compounded by inadequate educational programs. When those youth age and reenter the community years or decades later, they are further behind most people who never became justice involved. Recidivism happens when the formerly incarcerated are unable to compete for jobs with a livable wage, and a livable wage is rarely available to people without a higher education or advanced training in a trade. As such, recidivism is not just a result of bad decision making.

Anyone can make a bad decision, but everyone is not punished in the same way for the same bad decision. This is especially true of adolescents, whose underdeveloped brains make them more susceptible to negative peer influence and less able to anticipate future consequences for their actions. Martinson (1974), Di Iulio (1995), Congress, and mainstream media ignored this fact in the rise of penal populism. There was no discussion of the difference between adolescent and adult culpability, or environmental causes of crime.

It would take over a decade before the judiciary began to acknowledge juveniles are not really "super-predators". The Supreme Court, in *Roper v. Simmons* (2005), finally prohibited the execution of youths convicted of a crime if they were under 18 years of age when it was committed. The Court held a juvenile's reduced culpability "rendered suspect any conclusion that a juvenile falls amongst the worst offenders." Because their brains are under-developed, juveniles tend to engage in more "impetuous and ill-considered actions and decisions" and are "vulnerable to negative influences and outside pressures, including peer pressure." The immature and irresponsible behaviors of juveniles are a result of their underdeveloped brains, which means their conduct is not morally comparable to that of adults.

The impact of neuroscientific research on adolescent brain development continued. After the Court prohibited executing juveniles, it went on to ban mandatory LWOP sentences for juveniles. In *Miller v. Alabama* (2012), the Court held that "scientific findings-of transient rashness, proclivity for risk, and inability to assess consequences-both lessened a child's 'moral culpability' and enhanced the prospect that, as the years go by and neurological develop-ment occurs, [their] deficiencies will be reformed." Later, in *Montgomery v. Louisiana* (2016), The Court categorically banned life imprisonment "for all but the rarest juvenile … whose crimes reflect permanent incorrigibility."

The *Roper, Miller*, and *Montgomery* rulings were a "bright line" at which adolescents under eighteen received protection from America's harshest pun-ishments. The Court emphasized three characteristics demonstrated by research and common to human experience: adolescents are 1) immature, irresponsible, and impulsive; 2) vulnerable to external pressures and suscep-tible to peer influence; 3) still developing an identity and, therefore, can be rehabilitated (Bonnie, et al., 2013).

Neuroscience, a rapidly evolving domain of research, has shown that maturation of the brain structure, brain function, and brain connectivity, which includes executive function of the prefrontal cortex where decision making occurs, continues throughout a person's early twenties (Somerville, 2016). Leading adolescent development expert Dr. Laurence Steinberg con-ducted a 2009 study that found 18- to 21-year-olds are not fully mature enough to anticipate future consequences. In a widely cited longitudinal study, researchers at the National Institute of Mental Health (NIMH) tracked the brain development of 5,000 children, discovering their brains were not fully mature until at least 25 years of age. Like early adolescents, late adolescents (late adolescents are those in the teen years and the mid-to late-20s when the brain is in its final stages of development) struggle to avoid impulsive behaviors or understand the long-term consequences of their behavior (Dosenbach, et al., 2010).

Over 3,000 laws limit one's privileges and freedoms based on not achieving the age of twenty-one (Meggit, 2021). Since *Roper v. Simmons* (2005), purchase of tobacco and marijuana has been restricted to individuals aged 21 or older. Alcohol purchase already has such a requirement. Interstate commercial transportation, employment with federal law enforcement and most correctional agencies, professional licensures for any of the vocations taught in prison, and holding public office all require an individual to be 21 years of age or older. These are other restrictions signal a common understanding that "people under twenty-one lack maturity to hold occupations where their impulsivity or lack of foresight could pose a danger to others" (Meggit, 2021, p. 87).

As the 1983 and 1994 crime bills have shown, reason and science do not always govern the criminal legal system. If it did, penal experts would not have been ignored when Congress eliminated Federal Funding for college in prison programs. In the fever to address a crime wave, one that soon subsided, tough-on-crime laws led to the imprisonment of millions of men, women, and children. Prisons grew overcrowded, violent, and desolate without anything to counter the negative labeling and external pressures of American society. The real cost of apathy in the face of mass incarceration is measured in recidivism.

4

UNEDUCATED

A GED does not amount to much. For me, two years less than a high school diploma. Enough for the average menial labor job in a kitchen or at a construction site. Enough to fill out an application to a community college or state university.

A GED did not teach me how to save money, balance a checkbook, use a credit card, pay bills, establish a residence, register to vote, or be financially responsible. A GED did not teach me the importance of filing tax returns or how to file for government assistance. It did not help me organize a plan for the future. Other than get me out of MYC once, and certify I dropped out of high school when it was the most important place to be, my GED didn't feel generally equivalent.

Employment applications ask if an applicant has a GED, high school diploma, or any post-secondary education, but a lack of formal education was not necessarily a bar to employment for some jobs. On the surface it prevents economic mobility, which was part, but not all, of my problem. I was ignorant about a lot of things because I did not pay attention in school or listen to anyone who could have helped me. Now, when I needed that basic information, it was not there. More than anything, I discovered the education I had was wholly inadequate for creating an adult life.

I arrived in Asheville determined to get on my feet. My older sister and her husband took me in under the conditions I get a job and contribute to groceries. Her husband suggested a construction job, which wouldn't require experience, or an ID. It being January in the mountains though, the only places hiring people like me were restaurants in need of dishwashers, janitors, waiters, and the kind of jobs that can be taught to *anyone*. It didn't matter to me that I only qualified as a laborer, someone who would spend a lifetime of

DOI: 10.4324/9781003449454-6

40+ hour work weeks never advancing more than a few dollars past minimum wage, living hand-to-mouth, and having little to show for the effort. I never thought of myself as poor, or even homeless, but that is what my lack of skills and education amounted to, even if I was too ignorant and defiant to admit it to anyone, including myself.

Staying with my sister was temporary, though she gave no deadline to leave. She, too, had experienced addiction, knew the struggle, and invited me to stay with her when I called from Virginia. Her husband disliked the idea. After less than two months, he pressured her to kick me out, claiming I had ample time to get on my feet. Working as a dishwasher at Shoney's, I brought home about $120 per 35-hour work week at $5.25 an hour. Roughly $20 went to groceries every other week. Even if I had saved every penny, it might have amounted to a little over $800 in two months, but saving money had never been my strong suit. I left my sister's place with ten dollars.

On the street again, without regular transportation or a place to shower, I struggled to keep my job and finally, quit. Succumbing to a familiar pattern, I found ways to get high most days while living in a friend's barn and clinging to the idea of hitting the road again. Anything to forget the previous town's failures and draw hope from a new beginning. It remained just an idea. I continued to spiral out of control.

For the first time since the Maine Youth Center, I began cutting myself, severely enough that I recognized the need to get help. I called my sister and she took me to a hospital, which in turn sent me to another hospital with a wing for people who had mild-to-moderate mental health problems.

A voluntary hospital commitment implies a patient has enough self-control to seek or refuse help. Both the rehabilitation facilities I went to were considered voluntary for anyone not on probation. The primary principle is a desire or ability to change one's behavior. However, once in the hospital I didn't get better. Instead, I had a meltdown and became "acutely self-destructive," to the point where hospital staff placed me in isolation, restrained, sedated, and transferred me to a hospital more equipped to handle involuntary commitments. Tranquilized, in a strait jacket, I was beyond caring.

From the outside, Broughton Hospital looked more like a college campus with numerous ivy-covered, multi-story buildings, verdant lawns with towering oak trees and winding paved walkways cutting through the property. Nothing like what I imagined an asylum should look like.

On 104 Right, one of Broughton Hospital's locked wards (a section in which patients were not allowed to leave without an escort or drop in security level), they took my belt and shoelaces, started me on a regimen of psych meds, and constantly monitored me. Time disappeared. It grew difficult to remember hour-to-hour details. I slept a lot. Broughton was like every other institution: scheduled meals, group activities, and counselors for the mentally ill—people who cannot "get their shit together" for one reason or another.

An older blonde-haired man from Asheville was assigned to be my roommate. Among other things, he told me he had been committed for threatening to kill family members and neighbors, hearing voices that told him such things, and for alcoholism. We began hanging out together for the simple reason we were roommates, and both liked heavy metal music. At times he seemed more lucid and less "weird" than other patients on 104 Right, who ran a gamut of strangeness from gender dysphoria to severely schizophrenic and autistic patients who periodically required four-point restraints. None of them would have the same meteoric life-ending impact of my roommate.

There were red flags I ignored, that should have warned anyone who bothered to pay attention, that my roommate was dangerous. Hateful comments about other patients, stares levelled at female nurses and patients, violent fantasies, muttered rants ... I paid it no mind for several reasons. We were in a mental hospital, in a reasonably controlled environment, within shouting distance of one or more orderlies. I had my own problems and remained absorbed in my misery. My roommate also had access to pot and could buy alcohol from a store across the street from Broughton (leaving the property, which had no fences in 1997, was strictly forbidden, but not so strictly enforced since patients who reduced their levels were allowed more on-campus freedoms). Finally, I ignored most of my roommate's issues because I had, up to that point, been a poor judge of character, especially when it came to fitting in among "peers," overlooking immoral or even criminal behavior to assuage my desire for acceptance.

After two weeks of daily counseling and check-ups by a psychiatrist and psychologist, they diagnosed me with major depression, borderline personality disorder, polysubstance dependence, and poor impulse control. The psychiatrist said these diagnoses encapsulated my problems. To me, it was a bunch of jargon that did not show me any solutions to my problems. It did not change my situation and, regardless of any medication, I still felt hopeless and helpless.

In the end, all that mattered to the psychologist was bed space.

"You're not sick enough to be here," he said, then asked if there was somewhere I could go, someone willing to take me in and make sure I maintained outpatient treatment.

Defeated, I nodded.

Broughton Hospital discharged me into my sister's care who, with an older cousin from my dad's side of the family, found a place for me to stay. The older cousin decided I should be around people my age, getting her 17-year-old son and his roommates to put me up in their house. It was a mistake.

I slept on the couch and took my meds, looked for and got a job washing dishes, and tried to relax. The medications made thinking or planning impossible, leaving me dazed, high, and dizzy much of the time. This made simple tasks, like washing dishes, arduous. Maybe a different skill set could have helped me get a better job, but that would have required being in a place that taught those skills. MYC did not teach them. Drug rehabilitation partially taught them (the avoiding drugs part, anyway). Broughton Hospital could not even steer me in the direction of survival, expecting a homeless, uneducated delinquent with mental illness to keep up with outside appointments. I couldn't even find my way to a homeless shelter; what made them think I would make it to the outpatient center for check-ins and counseling, or come up with money to fill a medication prescription?

About two weeks into my stay on the couch, my 17-year-old cousin came home drunk one night and saw I too had been drinking. He didn't like it, or that he had been saddled with me by his mom and my sister.

"You're not supposed to be drinking!" he said and told me to leave if I wanted to drink.

I got up to get my bag, intent on finally hitting the road, when he attacked. My cousin was much heavier, and with surprise on his side it was not much of a fight. I struggled beneath him as he beat me. Then I broke.

Years later I would learn what happened next can be described as a psychotic break: a disassociation from reality and inability to conform my behavior to the law, caused by an eroded capacity to process stress and trauma, exacerbated by alcohol, pot, and the medications I consumed.

One moment my cousin was pummeling my face, the next I thrashed and screamed beneath him. It surprised him. His roommates called the police. When the police arrived, they cuffed me, slammed me against the cruiser, ripping one of two shirts I possessed, then stuffed me inside. As soon as the door closed, I repeatedly slammed my head against the metal partition between the front and back seats until my blood sprayed everywhere. By this time, I was screaming obscenities and waking up the neighborhood. Unlike the first time this happened in the hospital, where there were people trained to deal with such things, the cops left me in the back until an ambulance arrived. Then, they wrestled me out of the cruiser and onto the ground while I continued shouting and smacking my head against the asphalt. Eventually, the EMTs got me restrained, sedated, and to a hospital where they stitched me up before putting me back in Broughton.

It was late June 1997. Had I stayed in school I would have graduated that spring. High school felt like another world. A different galaxy from Broughton Hospital. A lifetime of self-destruction and instability, with my adult potential lying amidst the wreckage of my youth. The second trip to Broughton should have made it obvious I could not take care of myself at that time. Even though impulse, ignorance, immaturity, and addiction clouded my decisions, I knew I need the structure of an institution like Broughton to gain any sort of stability. My second involuntary commitment to a locked psychiatric ward should have left no questions.

Dysfunctional public institutions like the Maine Youth Center and Broughton Hospital do not suddenly become functional because a person needs them. They continue to fail in their responsibilities, then point to a limited number of success stories to distract their ineffective programs and process, or claim the problems are a lack of funding and, therefore, not their responsibility.

One of the many problems with a deinstitutionalized mental health system is that it never mattered that I lacked a family support system or stable place to live. It didn't even matter that under North Carolina law, after an involuntary commitment by the Sheriff's department, the hospital was *required* to keep me for 72 hours to ten days—the length of time needed to schedule a hearing to determine the duration of an involuntary commitment. Instead, Broughton's shrinks merely wanted to discharge me from the hospital no matter what the law stated or how much I needed to be there.

Within 24 hours of my second commitment, the psychologist gave me the freedom to leave 104 Right just about anytime I wanted during the day. He believed my only problem was that *I* chose to live in the wrong place. He then gave me his personal phone number and suggested we "get together" sometime in the future. There were rumors about this shrink hitting on patients; but until that moment it had been the kind of talk one hears about disliked staff in any institution. I made sure to lose the number in the nearest trash can.

The psychiatrist who did my intake screening and discharge during my first involuntary commitment changed up my medications—from an anticonvulsant to a tricyclic (antidepressant) and an antipsychotic. It was all the same to me. He agreed with the psychiatrist's assessment and signed my discharge papers, which would take a day to process.

The next day, while I waited for the paperwork to be done, I sat in front of the hospital's canteen (a place where patients on lower security levels congregated to use the vending machines, smoke, and talk) when I met a young woman several years older than me. She was bubbly and enthusiastic in conversation, talking about being in Broughton for cocaine addiction (which seemed odd, but I ignored it because I heard odd stuff all the time) and because her parents made her. She appeared normal, coherent, and interested in what I had to say. When she talked about her son I simply nodded and listened. Before I left, she scribbled her number on a piece of paper and stuck it in my pocket.

Fifty-six hours after my second involuntary commitment I was discharged into the custody of the Sheriff's department, who then brought me before a magistrate. The magistrate gave me an unsecured bond (no money down for release) on misdemeanor charges of resisting arrest and drunk and disorderly conduct. She told me to show up for court and they let me go.

I walked out of booking at the Buncombe County Jail bewildered and unsure what to do or where to go. For the first time, my homelessness really sank in. It was an isolating, lonely feeling. I called a friend and asked to sleep on his couch. His was the address I gave to the Broughton psychologist without any idea if he would allow me stay. He did so, albeit reluctantly. No one from the hospital or outpatient clinic bothered to follow up.

Within a few days I got a part-time job at the mall where my friend and his cousin worked. During my time off I sat in front of the mall's food court, smoking, or walked around. This is how I bumped into the woman I met at Broughton. She insisted on hanging out and, with nothing better to do, we picked up my roommate from Broughton because he would likely have alcohol and pot. Over the next week the three of us drank, smoked pot, and hung out together. Sometimes the woman brought her young son along.

I stayed inebriated, frequently blacking out and needing to be carried into my friend's trailer. The alcohol erased everything while the psych meds packed the hole in my head, where higher thought and decision-making should have occurred, with sawdust. Days and nights blurred together as I sought oblivion and found it.

Eight days after my second release from Broughton Hospital I was charged with the murders of the woman I met at Broughton and her young son.

My roommate from Broughton was charged with two counts of accessory to murder after the fact. Despite being labeled my "co-defendant" he never stood trial, having received a plea bargain for his "cooperation." Though there was an equal amount of physical evidence tying my co-defendant to commission of the murders, and a witnessed motive for the crimes, his release was set for 2010.

I was convicted of both murders and sentenced to death because, while under the influence of drugs, alcohol, and mental illness during an interrogation, I confessed to the crimes. There is no audio or video of the interrogation, which occurred under highly unusual circumstances.

As the transport van sped toward Central Prison my mind jumped over the evidence never developed and things never said or objected to at trial. I was angry and frustrated by the lack of defense presented by my trial attorneys, dumbfounded by their inability to talk to the jury about my co-defendant and his immunity from testimony despite being the sole "witness" to the murders. I wanted to scream and rage and weep—instead, I sat as wrapped up in thought as I was bound in chains, speeding toward my fate on death row.

One scene played in my mind more than the rest, and each time it pressed deeper into me. After the jury rendered its verdict, the judge pronounced my death sentence. A single word, never voiced but nonetheless present, struck my bones and reverberated in my thoughts. It defined my adolescence and would be the foundation of my life on death row. I heard it as surely as every other word that ended my life in the free world.

Failure.

5

THE OPPORTUNITY

Disquiet gnawed each of my thoughts in the back of the transport van, eating my focus as the landscape blurred past. Living surprised me much more than dying. It had been like this since the sixth grade, when an old man ran over and dragged me across an intersection beneath his car. From then on, I lived carelessly and erratically, slowly at first, but with increasing frequency and danger as adolescence took hold. Self-destructive behavior lent credence to an impending sense of doom, but so did multiple suicide attempts. Though I wondered about the afterlife of my Catholic upbringing, and sometimes sought THE END, this flirtation came from a place of frustration and ignorance. Death was not the problem; I knew nothing about life.

During the 20 months of my pretrial solitary confinement, I rediscovered reading. In school reading had been a chore, not something I wanted to do in my free time. Locked in a cell 23 hours a day for nearly two years, reading kept my mind tethered to reality even as I absconded through the pages of various books.

At the county jail, a milk crate held a dozen used paperback novels. I read them all several times, grateful for the rabbit hole they provided. Within them existed triumphs, joys, loves, and adventures I assumed were out of my reach. Even then, I hungered for something more substantive. During the darkest period of my incarceration, I needed to understand the "why" of my tumultuous life. I needed to know how to deal with the fact others wanted me to suffer and die. The answer came from history.

During WWII, Viktor Frankl, a Jewish psychotherapist, spent three years surviving the horrors of several Nazi concentration camps. From these experiences Frankl wrote *Man's Search for Meaning*, a book that illustrates what it takes to conquer any circumstance and find meaning in suffering.

DOI: 10.4324/9781003449454-7

Frankl wrote that suffering happens, is a part of human existence, but it can be borne if one finds purpose in it. What matters is how one responds. Would I succumb to my imprisonment, lose touch with civilization, and give up my humanity, or strive to give my life meaning and purpose, even on death row? Would I cower and complain or meet fate head on?

Comparing my circumstances to those of a concentration camp sounded disingenuous at best. My "suffering" was partly self-inflicted and certainly involved the threat of death, but it was not a daily threat. Frankl, however, didn't distinguish between types of suffering because suffering is a universal experience, regardless of the source, and can be approached with "the greatest of human freedoms": choosing one's attitude in any given set of circumstances.

If this advice came from a shrink in the free world who had endured little in the way of hardship, I would have scoffed at the idea of adjusting my attitude to overcome the circumstances. Frankl was not an ordinary psychotherapist asking patients to meditate or search their unconscious minds for answers: he faced certain execution every day against a backdrop of atrocities all the while imprisoned and starving.

Frankl never gave up or sought pity, he responded with resilience and cautious hope, focusing on the task of living. How could I ignore such a clear directive by a man who slept with death and awakened, did not allow bitterness or hatred to consume him, and provided brilliance in such a blinding absence of humanity?

Who was I to do anything less?

> Every day, every hour, offered the opportunity to make a decision, a decision which determined whether you would or would not submit to those powers which threatened to rob you of your very self, your inner freedom; which determined whether or not you would become the plaything of circumstance, renouncing freedom and dignity to become modeled into the form of a typical inmate?
>
> *(Viktor E. Frankl,* Man's Search for Meaning, *p. 75)*

I had only been on death row eight days, still trying to get my bearings, when Lowrider was executed. Not knowing him or what he looked like, it was hard to grasp the gravity of the event. In 1999, North Carolina's death row was crowded. New prisoners came in every few weeks as juries sentenced people to death at an ever-increasing rate. Because we were not locked down like other death rows, three double bunks clotted the dayroom, and 21 men filled cellblocks designed for 16. The night of Lowrider's execution, an officer sat on each block with instructions: stay out of the windows, do not try to communicate with the protesters outside, no extraneous noise or organized activities. Anyone in violation of these directives went to the hold. No exceptions.

With only a week in I still felt like an outsider, but not so much as to miss the brittle tension that filled the block. I did not have to know Low-rider or see him executed (executions occurred in another part of the prison and could only be viewed by a dozen select witnesses) to understand his fate would be mine. Sleep did not come that night and the cellblock was crypt quiet. I lay there wondering if all the executions would feel like this. Disconnected.

In the ensuing weeks and months, I occupied my time reading fantasy novels and occasionally exercising, with a steady diet of TV for the slower moments. Everyone was older than me in those days, and though I turned 21 shortly before trial, a number of guys referred to me as "new kid."

A middle-aged Native American man talked with me sometimes. Part Cherokee, part Apache, Chief told stories of doing time in the 70s and 80s, explained the nuances of prison politics and tried to teach me common sense. He was the first person to tell me that on death row there are people guilty of some horrendous crimes, but our time here would determine if that meant we are bad people too. Some are. Some are not.

"Everybody makes mistakes, cuz. But not everybody cares they made mistakes. Which are you?"

Chief commanded a great deal of respect from others, both because of the way he carried himself and for past exploits. A former Hell's Angel, he showed me that respect begins with taking care of yourself, but it's also as simple as manners, especially in prison. Except, in prison a lack of respect often means you fight. I discovered this a few months into my sentence.

My bunkmate, an older black man named Fly, tried me one night, testing to see how or if I would respond. Chief listened when I told him about the problem, then gave his advice. It might not seem like a big deal now, but this was Fly's way of testing young white boys. To see if he can turn them out. Make them his "boy." Go ask Bobby Jo how Fly works. He got turned out a few years ago. Maybe he wanted it. Who knows?

"The point, cuz, is what you do today will determine tomorrow. Make sure Fly knows what you think of being disrespected. Otherwise, it won't stop. It'll get worse and others will follow. Others who prey on weakness. It's your choice, cuz."

I refused to live the remainder of my time on earth being bullied or punked. Chief spoke the truth. It wasn't that I suddenly became a good judge of character, or openly trusted any advice given—what he said made sense. The fear felt in the moment of my response would never measure up to the shame and humiliation of being unwilling to stand up for myself. Changing my life meant responding to the circumstances of death row differently. There was nowhere to run, and I had to act with an eye toward the future. My time. My responsibility.

After I got out of solitary confinement for my fight with Fly, staff assigned me to a different block. I met Harvey there, the first of many friends who would be put to death, but not before sharing the best of himself with us.

Part of the advantage my fight with Fly carried is that he had been universally disliked by prisoners and staff. This earned me a small amount of credit from everyone. It also made people, like Harvey, more interested in helping me live above the negative influences that abound in prison. Harvey often spoke of his remorse and was vocal about his Christian faith on and off the block. Though regret tinged many of our conversations, he always urged me to pursue God.

"Ask your questions. Be angry. But be constant with Him."

We lifted weights together during outside recreation and it was on one such day they called Harvey to the warden's office and gave him an execution date.

Everyone stopped what they were doing when the death squad came for Harvey. A shift sergeant pushing a cart came on the block first, followed by the unit manager, a captain, and the warden. The sergeant would stay with Harvey on death watch, the final 72 hours of the condemned's life. Except for visits from family, clergy, and attorneys, that time would be spent in isolation and contemplation of the end. Harvey placed a plastic bag full of his personal effects on the cart. It would be picked up with his body.

We lined up to say goodbye, shaking Harvey's hand or giving him a hug. When my turn came, I stuttered a goodbye and hugged my friend. Harvey urged me not to let death row define my life in the way the State intended it. Recognize and accept my faults and be brave enough to grow past them.

"You have value," he said, tears staining dark cheeks. Harvey left with a wave, flanked by the guards.

Change in prison is difficult. It means discarding ingrained false beliefs, bad habits, and all the little lies we tell ourselves. It means accepting responsibility for your life and everything that happens in it. It means recognizing the system cares nothing about your humanity or potential to change but caring enough about yourself to change anyway. When mental illness is thrown into the process it becomes exponentially harder. My saving grace was a renewed interest in listening. My life before prison was an abject failure. Doing it my way, refusing to listen or acknowledge the need for help, ignoring the future, and seeking the approval of the wrong people walked me right up to the edge of the abyss and my own ignorance carried me to the bottom. It made sense to do the exact opposite upon making that discovery.

After Harvey's execution, Earl, a former Army drill instructor, got me into calisthenics. Earl accepted no excuses, tolerated no bullshit, pushed me hard, tested my limits, and showed me that with dedicated hard work I could build stamina and strength and confidence.

More than just exercise, Earl helped me grow up.

"It's easy to act tough in front of people," he said. "Who are you when nobody is watching? Who are you at night when that cell door closes? I'm the same Earl with everyone I meet, whether in prayer or on the block. God is my judge. I'm accountable to Him. Do you understand?"

Sometimes I did. Other lectures were lost in the dust of prison life and executions. I tried to absorb as much as possible, realizing Earl spoke about a lot of the same things my mom and dad had.

Earl possessed a number of qualities I never expected to find on death row. His honesty, forthrightness, pragmatism, and leadership lent him presence. Where Harvey admonished and joked, and Chief taught with stories and experience, Earl directed with logic and expected the best from everyone around him. Everyone sought his advice.

Despite the presence of these mentors my early years were spent learning not to hate myself. Reflecting on my brief life in the free world made that difficult. I continued to wrestle with anxiety, depression, and addiction, because even in prison there are ways to get high. Some days my hands shook so badly I could barely hold a spoon and it took both hands to write. My thoughts raced around the twin horrors of being unable to remember the murders or police interrogation that elicited my written confession, and the fact that not remembering is irrelevant. I was convicted and sentenced to death.

It would be several years before I learned about false confessions, ineffective assistance of counsel, and the substantial amount of undeveloped evidence that points to my co-defendant as the perpetrator of the murders, but none of that mattered in the moment. I still needed to awaken from the brainlessness of my youth, to cast away all the self-destructive habits that put me in the Maine Youth Center, rehab, Broughton Hospital, and prison. My problems began well before getting charged with murder, and to understand their origins and solutions I would have to analyze every poor decision. There were few good ones, and it would take time to untangle the mess of my adolescence.

Vigorous physical exercise became my foundation. This simple, independent activity allowed me to relieve much of my anxiety. As my body developed and self-esteem improved, at the urging of a prison shrink I quit taking psych meds. Despite an ever-changing carousel of pills, they left me lethargic, dependent on them for sleep, or made my skin crawl. As long as I took them, they would remain a crutch and temptation for abuse that did nothing to slow my self-mutilation.

Self-mutilation, which for me consisted of cutting or burning my arms and legs, is something I had dealt with off and on since the age of 11. I turned to it like the worst kind of drug, as if the pain could cut through the cloud of depression or calm my galloping thoughts. On death row the behavior continued as a way to pierce the mind-numbing fear of each execution, or much like a rubber band snap on the wrist, changed the downward spiral of my thoughts with stinging clarity.

Earl found out I had fresh cuts on my arms one day. At first, he looked at me in disbelief. But rather than turn away in disgust, he sat me down and told me not to do it anymore. Then Earl lectured on the need to respect my body like I respect other people. He urged me to rely on calisthenics and weight training as safe alternatives to self-abuse. Let exercise become a safe, comfortable place that allowed me to focus on reps and sets and the exertion put into a routine. Push everything else from my mind.

My mental illness was a battle over self-perception as much as a chemical imbalance. How could I fight to live if the act of self-harm showed I didn't value my life? Self-destructive, impulsive bad decisions were solvable. The path of my own personal hell should have been obvious. It had been there, waiting for me to grow strong enough to overcome the depression, anxiety, fear, addiction, ignorance, and negative peer influences. All I had to do was take responsibility for my life. Frankl provided the map. Chief, Harvey, and Earl were the guides.

After Harvey's execution I began attending the weekly Catholic Mass. Mom raised us in Catholicism, making sure my brother, sisters, and I attended Sunday school and were altar servers. When she fell out with the church we stopped going. We were not privy to her reasons, but as a teen I was more than happy to avoid church. On death row I returned to the church in an act of desperation and desire for answers.

At first, I listened. Eventually, when the priest asked our opinions about scriptural readings, I began asking questions, no longer able to stay quiet. What did Jesus write in the sand? Was Lazarus the first resurrection? Did Jesus know he was God? How could he be fully human and fully divine? My questions were combative, but Fr. Dan took them in stride, answering sometimes or calling me out if I didn't give something enough thought. There were six others who attended Mass back then, and four of us received Catholic Confirmation together in 2000. One of them, Mule, lived with me on the block and was both proud and excited when the Bishop conducted the ceremony.

In 2002, North Carolina's death row moved to a new building with more room. Only two executions were carried out that year, the lowest number since the early 80s. The following year, though, the State made up for its lapse by scheduling and carrying out seven executions between August and December. Three were my friends. One was Mule.

Mule's execution weighed as heavily as Harvey's had, despite all of those that came in between. His empty seat at Mass was a constant reminder. Scripture was already difficult to absorb, but with Mule gone, it seemed impossibly out of reach even as we all tried to go about the business of living on death row.

The following year, after an early September Mass, with two executions scheduled for October, we were discussing the Ascension when I asked Fr.

Dan a fairly blasphemous question about God, Jesus, and the Devil. The look on Fr. Dan's face and his response left me embarrassed and apologizing. Later, in Confession, Fr. Dan said,

"You're a bright guy, Lyle. I don't know how you got here, but it would be a shame to see you waste your potential. You need to get something on your mind. What would you say to enrolling in a college correspondence course?"

I looked at him. College? Me?

"I only have a GED," I said. "Besides, I dropped out of high school." Was he serious?

"A GED is enough. Does it sound like something that might interest you? Something to occupy your time, learn new things, and answer a few of your questions." He smiled at that and winked.

School had never been my forte, even when I did pay attention. Though I felt more mature at 26 than at 16, a decade had passed since high school. Could I still learn? Textbooks are a lot different from convict parables and prison norms. But I was hungry. Ravenous for something more than my stunted understanding of the world. Reading fiction killed time but was unfulfilling. I wanted more than to daydream and fantasize. I wanted to learn. Higher education meant freedom. Could I handle it?

The major difference between how I approached life on the street and how I approached it after seven years in prison was my willingness to listen. I had grown up on death row with the help of friends and beneath the pressure of executions. More than anything, I wanted to make sense of the "why" and "how" of my life and would do anything to achieve that. I recognized the opportunity before me and, for the first time, was ready for it. After some discussion I accepted Fr. Dan's offer of higher education.

It turned out to be the best decision of my life.

6

RETURNING TO THE CLASSROOM

The University of North Carolina at Chapel Hill, William and Ida Friday Center correspondence course catalog arrived in the mail late September 2004. I stood in the dayroom flipping through its pages as the din of shouted conversations and crack of dominoes slammed on the table washed over me. The catalog would distract from the coming executions in October, November, and December, taking my mind away to the world of academia for a brief visit. Accounting, biology, calculus, English, humanities, psychology—each course had a brief description, number of credit hours, prerequisites, required textbooks, and instructor's name. Some were more interesting—psychology and English—others less so—history and math.

I read the catalog like a best seller, not wanting to miss a single detail. An application detached from the back; with it I would need to send copies of my GED transcript and birth certificate since I had no other ID. Mom obtained the transcript and birth certificate, happy to help support something constructive with my time. Once Fr. Dan had these documents, he would mail them with the application and payment to UNC's Friday Center.

The course registration form looked much like a job application asking for the same mundane information, including whether an applicant had been convicted of a felony. The only struggle came in selecting my first college course. Fr. Dan said to pick something that interested me, but I needed to learn so many things. I wanted to unravel my past and understand my environment. College could answer my questions and teach me skills to create solutions, but I had to choose carefully.

One course description stood out above the rest, hinting at answers:

DOI: 10.4324/9781003449454-8

Social Interaction: an introduction to social psychological concepts that include relationships, peer groups, stereotypes, attraction and intimacy attitudes, and belief systems in the social environment.

I chose *Social Interaction*, but before mailing the application to Fr. Dan I had to get permission from Central Prison's Programs Department. At the time, the only "programs" on death row were religious services. Elsewhere in the prison a few other activities like a GED program, case management, and job assignments were orchestrated by the Programs Department, but little more than that. The Rec Department, a division within programs, actually had more to do with activities for the prison, holding the annual basketball tournament, showing weekly movies, and raising money for equipment through food sales. Writing a letter of request to the associate warden of programs should have been a simple first step on my journey to higher education, but I had never communicated with a "prison official" and doing so meant overcoming an ingrained prejudice against institutional authority.

During my confinement at the Maine Youth Center, staff physically and psychologically abused powerless juveniles. At Project Rebound, my first drug rehab, the director used demeaning and humiliating punishments—like putting a plate of food on the floor for a resident to eat like a dog if he wasted food—to keep us in line. Jailed for murder and sent to the Western Youth Institution for pretrial detainment, three staff beat and strangled me as a "welcome" to the notoriously abusive Morganton High Rise. Few institutional staff ever helped or were concerned with the welfare of their adolescent charges. None of them stopped the abuse.

Death row reinforced my belief institutional authority could not be trusted. Executions created a clear "Us vs. Them" line that should not be crossed, especially when the death squad (the warden, deputy warden, shift captain, unit manager, and a sergeant) escorted the condemned from his cell block to death watch. These prison officials represented the will of the State. Their job was to confine and end our lives. However polite and professional they may have been, it was difficult to see them as anything other than executioners, just as I am sure it was difficult for them to see us as anything other than convicted murderers. Our position relative to their punitive authority discharged communication.

Except, if I really wanted to learn, any aversion or bias against communicating with staff had to be put aside. I recognized the need to adapt because rigid, unthinking people—staff and prisoner alike—have the hardest time in life and prison. So, I wrote a polite letter to the associate warden of programs (AWOP) and asked permission to enroll in a correspondence course.

The following week the AWOP, Mr. Mac, called me to the unit sergeant's office. He granted my request and asked some questions about funding. With rare exceptions for pilot reentry programs, post-secondary education in North Carolina's prisons had to be funded by the prisoner through a private sponsor, though solicitation of that funding is prohibited.

"As long as someone extends the offer to you it's fine," he said.

Mr. Mac came from an era when prisoners could apply for federal Pell Grants. After access ended in 1994, and the educational apparatus in most prisons fell apart, people who supported education got pushed out of the system by more punitive-minded personnel. Mr. Mac was one of the few decent people left who believed prisoners need higher education and did what he could to be a facilitator.

Once the university sent my course materials, explained Mr. Mac, programs staff would bring them to me "to avoid any unnecessary hurdles within the mailroom restrictions on book size, or lengthy content reviews." The mailroom censors were often arbitrary in their book rejections, allowing the Holy Bible one moment and rejecting it the next. Mr. Mac understood this headache and policy gave him the authority to step around it for post-secondary education materials.

Mr. Mac encouraged in a way no other prison staff had in my experience, telling me to write him with any questions or problems.

"Just drop me a line when you're ready to take the exam and I'll have one of my staff take care of it." He looked at me then ducked his chin to peer over his glasses. "I'm old school, Mr. May. It's a shame they stopped funding college for you guys, that they made it political. That might be the worst thing the government could've done to y'all."

The *Social Interaction* textbooks and course syllabus arrived six weeks after Fr. Dan sent in the paperwork. I went to my cell and immediately began reading but only made it half a page before stopping to look up a word in the dictionary. I started reading again and made it a few paragraphs before stopping again to look up another word. The course was at the freshman level, my vocabulary was not. Studying would be a painfully slow process where the dictionary became an essential tool.

In the first lesson I learned how relationships and the depth of our communication with one another are influenced by the environment and belief systems. Almost immediately, I thought of writing the letter to Mr. Mac and how difficult it had been. How many people before me had succumbed to their prejudices and refused to interact with a group because of some negative experience or misconception?

Though the language of the textbook felt foreign—not what I found in *Harry Potter* or *Dune*, nor as mind-numbing as *Moby Dick*—I enjoyed studying the inter- and intra-relationships of dyads, triads, and groups. The text's authors referred to people as behavioral "targets" of interaction, which seemed curious, but reading examples helped me focus on a concept like "denigrating the target" and relate it to my experiences.

The course had 16 lessons, one for every chapter in the textbook, with five written assignments for each lesson. Because I spent several days reading, taking notes, and absorbing a chapter, the questions were not especially difficult. However, because the assignments had to be in pen with a carbon copy in case the lesson got lost in the mail, writing a one-page essay took a while.

College essays were a new experience. Up to that point I had only written letters to family and friends, asking for things every prisoner needs: love, support, understanding, and a connection to the outside world. As I wrote the essays, dictionary at hand for spelling, I kicked myself for dropping out of high school. It would not be the last time.

My heart sped when the first graded lesson came in the mail. Completely alone in the moment, standing in a dayroom full of people, I peeked in the envelope like a card player hoping for a good hand.

A signature in red ink, then a grade: A.

On the last page of the lesson, I found the instructor's only comment: "Welcome to the course. Superb job!"

My eyes stung. Evidence I wasn't stupid. Elation, pride, a sense of accomplishment—for the first time since my incarceration I felt good about something. The darkness, so immutable and impenetrable before now, had suddenly been pushed back.

Even with a self-imposed study schedule and healthy fear of failure, the prison environment does not make concentrating easy. Twenty to 24 prisoners lived on a block at any one time, and if only half of them were out in the dayroom, between their shouted raucous conversations, blaring announcements over the intercom, doors slamming open and shut, and one volume on the TV—loud noise is constant. I read in the morning while most people still slept and during the afternoon count when the entire prison locks down for 90 minutes. If this was not enough, I put in my earbuds and listened to classical music to drown out everything else.

Following the same process as before, I mailed in another lesson and received an A. Supportive and cautiously optimistic when I asked for help getting the GED transcript and birth certificate, my parents were overjoyed when they received the graded lessons. I sent them as proof that I took the opportunity of higher education seriously. The burden of proof would always be on me.

Within five months I completed the course's 16 lessons, receiving all As, and wrote Mr. Mac to request a proctor. The course syllabus stated that exam preparation should involve reviewing chapters, graded assignments, and any instructor comments. To pass the course students must pass the exam.

If studying social psychology and preparing for my first exam in a decade were the only things on my mind it might have been easier. Earl had an execution date coming up. My friend and mentor would be strapped to a gurney and put to death in front of a small group of witnesses like some seedy peepshow in the red-light district, with half the people horrified and the other half satisfied. This image blotted out every other in my mind until studying for any length of time became impossible.

In the brittle, hollow moment after an execution, giving in to despair feels natural. Who can fight the power of the State? Fatalism is as constant as the noise and just as damaging but developing ways to resist it is just as essential to maintaining sanity over time. The correspondence course was a tool to chip away at the sense of impending doom; a tool to shove back the force of night, a tool I promised to wield with all my might.

Exam day arrived without notice.

A programs staff member called me to the office and said, "Are you ready?"

She had been on death row before, passing out books, but seemed surprised that anyone was enrolled in a college course. She took me to an office typically used by prison shrinks and handed me a sealed envelope. Three hours to complete 16 essays. I looked at the woman, who was signing the proctor's form.

"Something wrong?"

I had spent hours writing one essay for a lesson, now there were 16 in three hours?

"No. Just nervous. I've never done this before."

Sweating, pencil in tightened fist, I began writing. As a teenager, I failed to grasp the importance of having an education. Sitting in an office on death row, everything changed. Before, I stood blind and ignorant at the edge of an abyss but kept walking. At the bottom of that abyss on death row, where everyone scrabbled for purchase against impossibly steep sides, I understood education had always been the answer. Taking a college correspondence course was never about occupying my mind but transforming it.

Four weeks after sending in the exam, a final course report arrived in the mail. I snatched it out of the envelope and stared at the yellow sheet of paper. A combined lesson and exam grade for the total course grade: A. The instructor left a comment:

"Outstanding work, Lyle! Your essays demonstrated great understanding of the material. Best of luck in all your future endeavors."

Having proven myself capable, I showed the course report to Fr. Dan and asked to enroll in another course. He agreed.

Choosing an introductory psychology course felt like the best way to begin the hard work of understanding my adolescence. Now more than ever I needed to learn about myself, capital punishment, and all of the elements composing my world. *General Psychology* seemed to hint at such answers, its catalog description promising an in-depth look at human behavior through theory, experiment, and critical thinking. The most profound part of the psychology textbook was each chapter's conclusion with critical thinking skills. Rather than just teach students psychological concepts, it helped foster awareness through observation, analysis, and questions. The discussion on logical fallacies so enthralled me I taped a list of them to my shelf like some talismanic script meant to banish ignorance. Among the many critical thinking skills, I learned how to write essays for exams and tricks to reduce indecision for multiple choice tests. Choosing psychology signaled an official end of tolerance for the brainlessness that destroyed my life.

I withdrew from the day-to-day bustle of prison life, strictly limited my TV watching, avoided gambling, getting high, circular conversations, and wasting time. My vocabulary improved, though not because I used psychological jargon or pretentions words in random conversations. I continued studying, turning in lessons, and learning.

After acing *General Psychology*, Fr. Dan wanted me to enroll in two courses. I chose *Writing and Rhetoric* and *Personality Psychology*. Where *Writing and Rhetoric* promised to sharpen my communication skills, *Personality Psychology* helped me dig deeper into my identity and understand the idiosyncrasies of others.

The success of my routine, interest, and dedication made me more confident. I read and reread chapters, took extensive notes, completed assignments more quickly and began to feel competent for the first time in my life. My first C came from the *Writing and Rhetoric* instructor. Rather than shake me, fear of failure spurred me on, though it did little to close the gap between what college level English requires and a GED teaches. Grammar, syntax, and sentence structure often seemed more difficult than understanding long-term potentiation in neural pathways or personality measures. I overused idioms and disliked analyzing Shakespeare. My infatuation with psychology, though, had met with a healthy dose of reality: I had a lot to learn.

References

Alexander, M. (2010). *The New Jim Crow: Mass Incarceration in the Age of Colorblindness*. The New Press.

Baumgartner, F. R., Daniely, T., Huang, K., Johnson, S., Love, A, May, L., Mcgloin, P., Swagert, A., Vattikonda, N., & Washington, K. (2021). Throwing away the key: The unintended consequences of tough-on-crime laws". *Perspectives on Politics*, 19(4), 1233–1246. doi:10.1017/S153759272100164X.

Bonnie, R. J., Johnson, R. L., Chemers, B. M., & Schuck, J. A. (Eds) (2013). *National Research Council Reforming Juvenile Justice: A Developmental Approach*. National Academy Press.

Di Iulio, Jr., J. J. (1995, Nov. 27). The coming of the super-predator. *The Weekly Standard*, 23.

Dosenbach, N. U., Nardos, B., Cohen, A. L., Fair, D. A., Power, J. D., Church, J. A., Nelson. S. M., Wig, G. S., Vogel, A. C., Lessov-Schlaggar, C. N., Barnes, K. A., Dubis, J. W., Feczko. E., Coalson, R. S., Pruett, J. R. Jr, Barch, D. M., Petersen, S. E., & Schlaggar, B. L. (2010). Prediction of individual brain maturity using fMRI. *Science*, 10(329), 1358–1361. doi:10.1126/science.1194144.

Feeley, M. M., & Simon, J. (1992). The new penology: Notes on the emerging strategy of corrections and its implications. *Criminology*, 30(4), 449–474. doi:10.1111/j.1745-9125.1992.tb01112.x.

Goodman P., Page J., & Phelps M. (2017). *Breaking the Pendulum: The Long Struggle over Criminal Justice*. Oxford University Press.

Johnson v. Texas, 509 U.S. 350, 367 (1988).

Kappeler, V. E., & Potter, G. W. (2018). *The Mythology of Crime and Criminal Justice* (5th ed.). Waveland Press.

Lawrence, D. L. (1994) The scope and diversity of prison higher education. In Williford, M. (Ed.), *Higher Education in Prison: A Contradiction in Terms?* (pp. 32–51). Onyx Press.

Martinson, R. (1974). What works? Questions and answers about prison reform. *Public Interest*, 35, 22–54.

Meggit, A. (2021). Trends in laws governing the behavior of late adolescents up to age 21 since Roper. *Journal of Pediatric Neuropsychology*, 7(1–2),74–87. doi:10.1007/s40817-40021-00102-0.

Miller v. Alabama, 132 S. Ct. 2455 (2012).

Mistretta v. United States, 488 U.S. 361 (1989).

Page, J. (2004). Eliminating the enemy: The import of denying prisoners access to higher education in Clinton's America. *Punishment in Society*, 6(4), 357–378.

Somerville, L. H. (2016). Searching for signatures of brain maturity: What are we searching for? *Neuron*, 92(6), 1164–1167. doi:10.1016/j.neuron.2016.10.059.

PART 3

The Intrinsic Value of Higher Education: Resilience and Resistance

In the early 19th century, penal reformers reinvested in the idea that intense discipline and punishment, coupled with moral instruction and labor, would force prisoners to "repent" their crimes and reform their behavior. With parole as inducement, this formula became the core of the rehabilitative element in the penal system. Over time, religion played less of a role and was joined by psychotherapeutic programming, vocational training, and higher education. Crime became less a moral failing and more a psychological and educational one.

By 1983, the penal system was profoundly changed when the inducement of parole ended: truth-in-sentencing required prisoners to serve 85% of their sentence; mandatory minimums increased the average sentence length and removed judicial discretion; three-strikes-laws further punished repeat offenders; and life without parole (LWOP) sentences were handed down for numerous crimes. With the rehabilitative ideal rejected by the Senate and U.S. Supreme Court, prisons grew draconian and overcrowded. Then came the 1994 Omnibus Crime Bill, which spawned the prison industrial complex; the 1995 Prison Litigation Reform Act (PLRA), which made it much harder for pro se prisoners to sue over conditions of confinement; and the 1996 Antiterrorism and Effective Death Penalty Act (AEDPA), which greatly eroded federal judicial oversight of unconstitutionally lengthy sentences handed out by state courts. The era of human warehousing had arrived.

Prison conditions across the country grew cruel and unrelenting, compounded by an influx of guards and prison officials who interpreted America's "tough-on-crime" stance to mean merciless correctional brutality. The public, in a moral panic after consuming a steady diet of media sensationalism and crime dramas, were misled into believing "justice" means people sent to prison deserve to suffer because of their criminal convictions, do not deserve the "privilege" of higher

DOI: 10.4324/9781003449454-9

education, and that rehabilitative programming is a waste of taxpayer dollars. Leaving behind rehabilitation meant returning to retributive justice. Super max prisons with little human contact, years-long stints in solitary confinement for tens of thousands, restraint chairs, tasers, beatings and more executions-all out of the public's view, but with its implicit acceptance.

Retributive justice fomented greater levels of prison violence when basic health, safety, and security needs were not being met after most incentives for good behavior were removed. Researchers explained violence through deprivation, importation, and integration. The deprivation model of penal violence focuses on how culture and penal policy make access to basic resources difficult and inconsistent (Johnson et al., 2017). Lack of space became a steadily increasing problem ignored by courts and exacerbated by gangs. Victor Hassine (2011), a law school graduate serving life without parole in Pennsylvania, described the effect of deprivation:

> By 1982, Graterford's general population rose to over two thousand. Every cell in the general population blocks was occupied.... There were not enough jobs to go around so men sat idle on B-Block. This resulted in more theft, which in turn led to more fights and more stabbings.... As thievery increased, gangs flourished ... C- and D-Blocks were virtual war zones. There were so many fights and retaliations that guards were getting injured in the melees.
>
> *(p. 74)*

The importation model of penal violence focuses on pre-prison characteristics such as age, sex, gender, prior victimization, ethnicity, demographics, socio-economic status, prior employment, and educational level (Johnson et al., 2017). Hassine (2011) described violence imported from the street and its influence on the penal environment:

> Fear and violence changed Graterford as profoundly as it has changed me. The new prison subcultures with their disrespect for authority, drug addiction, illiteracy, and welfare mentality had altered the institution's very character. All the evils of the decaying American inner city were being compressed into one overcrowded prison. Ironically, the violence that had long been a tool of control by the administration was now being used against it to send the prison system hurtling out of control.
>
> *(p. 71)*

A more integrative approach to penal violence incorporates individual characteristics, institutional deprivation, and situational factors such as water outages, food shortages, or pandemics. Research has found that under-educated younger males from dysfunctional or abusive families, who have a prior history of victimization or violence, or live in low-income neighborhoods are more likely to commit violent acts in prison (Johnson et al., 2017). Increasing this likelihood are gangs, ineffective penal management, understaffing, a lack of incentives for good behavior, work, and rehabilitative programs (Johnson et al., 2017).

In 2004, the public got a chance to see what had come from its support of retributive justice. A series of pictures revealed former American prison guards-turned soldiers were torturing Iraqi POWs at Abu Ghraib prison (Gottschalk, 2015). The abuses at Abu Ghraib may have disgusted some military commanders and shocked the public, but corrections officials understood it was it was institutionalized violence: guards were agents of the prison, suspending moral restraints that keep individual acts of violence in check, then carrying out physical and psychological acts normalized in the penal environment despite being abhorrent to civilized society (Johnson, et al., 2017). Double and triple celling prisoners, taunting those in pain, denying medical aid to those in need, and confining suicidal prisoners to 3ft x 3ft "squirrel cages"—a space smaller than many in animal shelters—were also practices revealed at Abu Ghraib that are common in U.S. prisons (Louisiana Sheriff Cages, 2011).

Prison conditions and the threat of brutality have a heavy effect on the attitudes, beliefs, and behaviors of the incarcerated. Forced labor, no meaningful programs or positive reinforcement, and an emotionally toxic, violent environment makes prison criminogenic (i.e., prisoners become more likely to commit crimes than before) (Gibney, 2019). This alone suggests the penal system fails on its own terms. Prison was meant to reduce crime, not create it. Yet, when many of the tiny freedoms people take for granted are punished as an illicit activity in prison, the institution necessarily becomes criminogenic (Butterfield, 2004; Herbert, 2004). The prisoner automatically finds a way to circumvent senseless, arbitrary policies, especially if it eases the crushing weight of incarceration in a dangerous environment.

In the normalcy of exceptional brutality, the incarcerated are left groping in the dark absence of rehabilitative programs to engage in personal growth. The penal system is designed for personal failure because many of the tools once available for mature coping were removed. In addition to harsh conditions of confinement, most prisoners have impulse control and relational problems, cognitive deficits, and limited coping skills (Zamble et al., 1984 cited in Johnson et al., 2017). This does not even account for the mentally ill, who comprise over 21% of the carceral population and are significantly underserved (Hurley, 2018). Prison, in fish-bowl-like fashion, magnifies these problems and deficits, creating difficult, stressful situations for people who already struggle to make effective decisions. Their inability to cope, claim Zamble et al. (1984), is the "central cause of the maintenance and repetition of criminal acts" (cited in Johnson et al., 2017, p. 64). Inmate coping is demonstrated in a lack of self-control, an inability to set and reach goals, plan and organize activities, or develop a positive work ethic (Zamble et al., 1984).

Higher education is a mature coping mechanism (more so than vocational training) that teaches organizational, critical thinking, and time management skills, self-discipline, and personal accountability. Each trait is important, but more than most, accountability should be what society wants incarcerated people to develop. The intrinsic value of higher education in prison goes beyond becoming a contributing member of society, obtaining a good job, or effectively managing one's incarceration. Higher learning fosters resilience-the capacity to regain personal power and a strong sense of self in the face of severe hardship or adversity (Ford, 2010, cited in Bartollas & Schmalleger, 2014). Some experts suggest everyone is born with an innate capacity for resilience, which, if true, means it can be developed through the right kind of education. Similarly, higher learning also cultivates problem-solving skills, a sense of purpose, critical consciousness, independence, and responsibility (Rodman, 2007, cited in Bartollas & Schmalleger, 2014).

Leaving prison does not mean surviving prison if one remains attached to the criminal legal system and, like a yo-yo, eventually returns. Under some circumstances, the collateral consequences of a felony conviction are to blame. Yet, nothing speaks more clearly of systemic penal failure than an average national recidivism rate of 700,000 people per year (Johnson et al., 2017). Approximately 87% of all prisoners (the remaining 13% are life and death sentenced prisoners, and this total percentage does not include people who die in custody each year) will one day get out. Two thirds of that number are rearrested for post-release supervision (technical) violations or committing new crimes, with over half reincarcerated within three years of release (Visher, 2007). Since most people in prison have release dates, it is imperative they receive unfettered access to, and are encouraged or gain incentives to participate in, PSCE programs. Individuals who participate in PSCE programs while incarcerated are approximately half (47.49 %) as likely to recidivate compared to those who do not. The risk of recidivism declines even more with every level of degree earned.

Despite the numerous benefits, a reentry focus greatly limits who can access PSCE programs. While most prisoners get out, few have access to PSCE programs. Though the 2008 Second Chance Act (not to be confused with the 2015 Second Chance Pell pilot program) provided grants for prison education and rehabilitation. The annual budget never exceeds $100 million per year, which amounts to about $50 per prisoner (Gibney, 2019). Most states do not fund PSCE programs and only a smattering of non-profit organizations do. The result is that prison officials restrict access to PSCE programs to people nearing release, which undermines the ameliorative effect they can have on the penal environment.

Providing open prison education programs can counter institutional violence and criminality by training more of the incarcerated people to be positive role models engaged in productive pro-social activities. Such positive modeling has a normative effect over time that leads to legitimate compliance with the law (Tucker, 2009). The incarcerated student needs to learn how to resist the negative influence of drugs, gangs, and obstructionist prison policies, all of which create a nexus that maintain the carceral state. Higher education thwarts that influence via the skills students develop and academic success. Moreover, educational programs keep incarcerated students positively engaged, focused on achieving valuable goals, and constantly working toward a more balanced, socially conscious identity (Worth, 1995). Higher education is about higher thinking. Harvard University President Drew G. Faust once wrote:

> Education liberates the mind, even when the body is oppressed. It gives us perspective as a passport to other times, other places, and other points of view, as well as a way to learn about ourselves and to reimagine our lives in ways that alter us forever.
>
> *(cited in Arjini et al., 2018)*

President Faust also described higher education as "the civil rights issue of our time" (cited in Arjini et al., 2018). This speaks not only to the fundamental worth of every human being, but the intrinsic value of higher education. As a right provided to anyone in prison who decided to pursue it, PSCE programs would significantly improve the weak social bonds that lead to crime, and help more people become "free-thinking, independently minded and humane citizens that constitute the foundation of a genuine democratic society" (Tucker, 2009, p. 108).

Providing incarcerated people an unrestricted avenue to higher learning so they can reach their fullest potential as human beings does not diminish the hard work of law-abiding citizens who cannot afford college or reward crime. In treating higher education as a right that anyone can and should access, it levels the social field and removes many of the barriers that keep the marginalized on the fringes of society. Higher education, then, is not a panacea so much as it is the greatest equalizer in the living world.

Higher education is valuable specifically because of the autonomy it provides students, an essential tool for people in and out of prison. However, for anyone in confinement, separating from the institutional environment, discovering one's identity apart from it, learning how to overcome obstacles rather than being consumed by them, thinking outside the box, and challenging negative stereotypes is imperative to survival. Prison helps no one, neither the people within nor those on the outside, but higher education does so by empowering the oppressed. It is a key to unlock any gate—no matter who keeps it.

7

CHOOSING HIGHER EDUCATION

The staff "break room," across the hall from the Unit 3 sergeant's office, had once been a barber shop, waiting room for strip searches and urinalysis, and storage room. Two large plexiglass windows allow passersby to see inside the room even when the lights are off. Before the night of an execution the break room is closed, two long tables hug the wall laden with Solo cups, plastic forks and spoons, paper plates, napkins, bottles of soda, oversized bags of chips, cookies, cold cuts, and a large sheet cake colorfully decorated with frosting. The celebratory meal is displayed to every death row prisoner walking by it on the way to the chow hall. Denials from staff that the food was for a celebration fell flat. Birthday cake is an odd snack the night of every execution, unless you are the executioner.

The cramped office where I usually took my exams held a shrink and a schizophrenic prisoner who often had conversations with the wall or stood stock still staring into space. Ms. Nance, a young woman from the programs department appointed as my proctor for the *Personality Psychology* exam, asked the shift sergeant if I could use the break room.

I cringed.

I didn't want to take my exam in the break room, knowing what it had been used for on any number of occasions. Bad enough the door would be left open, officers walking up and down the hallway while their radios squawked and squealed, keys jingling and boots squeaking. If a chow group came through and lingered in the hall, concentration would be impossible. The break room had to be one of the worst places to take an exam, but no other rooms were available.

I put it out of my mind, showed Ms. Nance how to fill out the proctor's form, and began the exam. Three hours and 200 multiple choice questions.

DOI: 10.4324/9781003449454-10

Personality theories, measures, experiments, longitudinal studies, disorders—a comprehensive review of the textbook. As with any psychology course it was difficult not to analyze myself. Introverted, open to experience, mostly conscientious and somewhat agreeable, maybe even a bit neurotic to account for being anxious. Mom is a worrier and I got it from her—no genetic deviance there. Each trait represented a host of behaviors and social interactions, with every personality scale measuring variation in those behaviors.

A third of the way into the exam, I overheard a correctional officer and the sergeant talking.

It had been reasonably quiet until the CO said, "I can't wait 'til the next one. I just want to see it happen."

The sergeant muttered a reply about executions being on hold.

"Well," said the CO, "whenever they schedule the next one, I want to watch."

I cursed, wishing the hallway filled with people. The exam page blurred, words swimming in orderly waves. "I want to watch" echoed through my mind. Some might have quit in that moment. Stormed into the office and screamed on the CO and escalated the situation. It mattered little whether he forgot I sat barely 15 feet away in the break room or intended me to hear. My face burned as if slapped.

Every morning awakened me to the reality of life on death row. Every morning, I made a conscious choice to do and be more than just another "inmate" or some guy in prison, resisting the mindless violence of prison norms and pushing back against ignorance—others' and my own. I did not suddenly think college correspondence courses would convince a judge or governor to spare my life. I sat in the break room where some staff reveled in the death of people, I grew up around, listening to another boldly speak of wanting to watch an execution, because I wanted to learn. Nothing would dissuade me from that purpose.

A month after the *Personality Psychology* exam was mailed, my grade report came back with an A.

That fall, I enrolled in and aced an introductory philosophy course and *English Composition*. UNC Chapel Hill's Friday Center did not offer degrees through correspondence and had a limited course selection. A friend told me about Ohio University, explaining their long history of providing accredited correspondence degree programs to prisoners. Earning a degree two courses at a time seemed unlikely on death row, but a de facto moratorium on executions went into effect in 2007 while issues about the execution protocol were litigated in court. The moratorium turned uncertain death sentences (only one in five prisoners sentenced to death in North Carolina have actually been executed since 1972) into uncertain life sentences. I would continue fighting to have my conviction and sentence overturned, but appellate court relief could not be guaranteed. Nor could I be sure the church would fund correspondence courses that long.

Both of these things were out of my control. Judges are fickle. Laws change. Church sponsorship might continue. The future is fluid. Ten years before I never imagined enrolling in a college course, let alone completing six and considering pursuing a degree. I wrote to Ohio University's Haning Hall and requested their correspondence course catalog.

Ohio University's College Program for the Incarcerated offered several associate's and one bachelor's degree program. According to the catalog, completion of an associate in arts degree required an accumulation of 60 credit hours, the majority of which had to be earned through OU. My credits from UNC Chapel Hill would count toward that number, so I mapped out which courses I wanted to take, and which were general education requirements. Despite liking psychology and writing, I needed applied science, humanities, and mathematics courses to complete an AA degree with a social science emphasis. Excited, I hoped to be able to convince my sponsor.

The offer of college correspondence courses began with Fr. Dan, but he transferred to another parish and Fr. Mark took his place. I did not take their kindness or the church's generosity for granted. Each course presented an opportunity to learn and "fill the hole in my head" as dad used to say, but it also made me responsible for the investment, even if the church and priests intended it as a gift. The reciprocity seemed implicit: do well and we will support you.

When I next spoke with Fr. Mark after Mass, I asked about switching to Ohio University, handing him the course catalog.

"As long as the church is willing and able, I'd like to continue my education. But rather than just enroll in random courses and collect credits, I want to work toward something, even if it's slowly."

Fr. Mark looked at the catalog, waiting until I finished.

"What you say makes sense and it seems like Ohio can offer you greater opportunities. Let me discuss this with someone at the church. Which courses do you want to enroll in?"

"Basic mathematics, since it's a requirement, and *Introduction to Sociology* because it's a prerequisite for higher level sociology courses."

Later that night, lying on my bunk half-daydreaming, half-reading Malcolm Gladwell's *Tipping Point*, I imagined earning a degree and how different it would be. Up to this point, my course selection focused on subjects applicable to my incarcerated life. That would change some with degree requirements. Science and math were not my strongest subjects in school—could I do as well in them as psychology? Also, before, learning had been enough, lessons and exams attainable, short-term goals. They could be difficult sometimes, but not impossible. Pursuing a degree meant reaching for something in the distant future. It meant imagining a future in a place where hopes and dreams are entombed alongside human potential. It meant defying the odds.

Fr. Mark gave me permission to enroll in Ohio University courses, but any further communication about school would be with someone at the church who oversaw community programs. This would remove any sign of impropriety since prison policies forbade solicitation, favoritism, fraternization, or undue familiarity with staff or volunteers like the priests. Though approval for the courses came from the church pastor, the church was my sponsor.

A letter from an academic advisor arrived shortly after my registration for the math and sociology courses. She welcomed me to Ohio University and explained the associate degree program, adding that if I needed help to write her with any questions. After receiving my UNC Chapel Hill course transcript, my advisor sent a DARS (Degree Audit Report System) printout, which tracks progress toward graduation by listing credits attained and needed, GPA; pre-approved "tier" courses for freshmen sophomores, juniors, and seniors; general education requirements, electives and area of concentration (AOC) requirements. My AOC was social sciences.

A month later, the programs director under Mr. Mac, Ms. Powell, brought me a box with the textbooks, course syllabi, and a number of pens, pencils, pads of paper, prepaid business envelopes, and two folders. Small things like postage and writing materials make a difference in prison. It also felt good to know the university recognized this. Higher education is hard enough without having to scrounge for extra pencils.

Basic math included a review of algebra, fractions, word problems and the like, so I finished the lessons quickly. Introductory sociology explained influences on human behavior in the social environment, organizational structures, and numerous theories. I began to understand how structuralism explains bureaucracy and the inner workings of institutions. While colloquialisms may have described prison pecking orders among staff, or how "shit rolls downhill," neither improved understanding. Where psychology helped me grasp internal origins of behavior, sociology lent comprehension of the penal system, prison norms and mores, and my place within society. UNC Chapel Hill courses had single, comprehensive exams that covered the entire textbook—OU courses had mid-terms and finals. The inclusion of a mid-term reduced the weight of the final, and while passing both was necessary to passing the course, it proved enormously helpful over time.

After finishing math and sociology, I felt confident and competent enough to request three courses. It would require juggling more reading, assignments, and exams, but it's not like I had a job or other activities getting in the way. There were no rehabilitative programs on death row. An hour of outside recreation and a 100-yard walk to and from the chow hall three times a day was the only scheduled movement. Outside of considerable noise distractions, and the occasional high school drama on the block, nothing but my own shortcomings would prevent the completion of three courses. Ordinary college students often double that number, have many more distractions and anxieties, and still get it done. I had a lot of catching up to do.

Prison provides plenty of time for self-reflection and analysis. In the free world, immaturity, drugs and alcohol, anxiety and depression, and ignorance retarded my ability to resist negative peer influence or even survive. Out of the fog of substance abuse and mental illness, armed with critical thinking skills, and mentored by people who had faced the same problems as me, I was able to mature. I now recognized the potential my parents and teachers spoke about, and this awakening demanded daily accountability. I would not create excuses for myself or be okay with the low standard of doing well for someone in prison. That kind of thinking smacked of constraints on my potential, as if achieving beyond prison walls or labels could not be done.

The three courses I chose—*Critical Approaches to Fiction, Human Biology,* and *The Social Psychology of Justice*—arrived in late August. Ms. Powell designated Ms. Jay to bring me the materials and proctor exams.

"Well, look at you, Lyle May! What kind of degree are you seeking?" Ms. Jay was a short, Asian woman with a dry wit who could never gain rank in the good old boy prison administration because she refused to play politics. Or, as she told me, "I don't kiss the right amount of ass and have more education than the warden." Ms. Jay used to bring around outside library books and art supplies ordered and purchased by prisoners from an outside vendor. Both programs were discontinued by 2005 for obscure reasons that changed with each telling but could be attributed to punitive-minded wardens who care nothing about programs. Though Ms. Jay wanted us to have programs, she had no power to implement them, and asking to create learning opportunities under an anti-program prison administration had likely already cost her promotion opportunities. It made my access to higher education invaluable and in constant danger of being eliminated. I told Ms. Jay about the associate degree program through Ohio University and she nodded, saying she would help however she could.

I enjoyed all three of the new subjects, delighting in how the knowledge helped me think more broadly about the world and make better decisions. *Social Psychology of Justice* explored the juncture where psychology and the criminal justice system meet. Interrogations, coerced confessions, criminal profiling, eyewitness fallibility, jury dynamics, insanity, and diminished capacity defenses, lie detector test inadmissibility, and more. The course dug into many legal concepts central to my own case, processes never explained or discussed by my incompetent trial attorneys. I read the textbook closely, searching for answers but only discovering more questions.

The first two mid-term exams—English and biology—arrived the same day. Ms. Jay allowed me to take one before lunch and one afterward. For the biology exam, I sat in an empty office used by the prison shrink three days a week. Sitting behind the desk felt strange, like going back to visit your grade school and realizing everything is much smaller than you remember. Adding to that out-of-place feeling, the bottom floor recreation group came in from outside, filing past and looking in the office to see me hunched over the desk, writing. Most of them knew I took college courses. Some encouraged me and were even proud, others not so much. At one point or another, they saw me taking an exam because there are no quiet, out-of-the-way places on the unit for a proctored test.

The group passed and a few guys called my name, said hello, or half-mocked, "College boy!" and "Look at the professor!" I did my best to ignore it until one loudmouth said, "What he gonna do wit dat education on the gurney? Ain't no good less it get him outta prison. I be damned I waste all that money ..."

Finishing the exam became difficult. My mind locked on the negative comment. I grew angry and struggled with questions about RNA and white blood cells. My hand shook. Was he right? Was I wasting time and the church's money? Even after finishing the exams, glad to be done, doubt about what I was doing began to eat at me.

Several weeks later when mom visited, she sensed something wrong. "You've got something on your mind. What is it?"

"Am I wasting my time, mom?" It hurt to voice it after investing so much effort. "Who am I to get a degree on death row? Why should I bother if they're going to execute me?" I hated myself in that moment for voicing the fatalism common on death row.

Her mouth thinned into a straight line. I remembered the no-nonsense look from my childhood.

"Do you like learning?" she asked and placed her hand on the plexiglass between us. I mirrored her. "My son, you have to do what makes you happy, or what brings you peace. You have done so well in a place with virtually nothing. Your father and I are proud of how far you've come. We can see the change. Who else is doing what you are?"

"On death row? I don't know. Probably more if they had the chance."

"That's not the point. You chose to make the most of your time. Chose to grow up when you could have given up. Chose to ignore the naysayers. They'll always be there. The church is supporting you because they see your potential. If it leads to a degree, then great. If not, it hardly matters. You took the most important step, now take another and another and another. Keep making the most of this opportunity and who knows what will come of it? Only good."

Choosing higher education had always been more than a means to an end. It began as something to do other than watch TV all day, slap dominoes or cards on a table, get into trouble, and fantasize in the pages of some novel. The circumstances of my incarceration may be muddled and inexplicable, but that did not mean I had to wallow in my own ignorance. My *bildungsroman* was a transformational journey both arduous and lonely, but one that would take me far beyond prison walls and ordinary expectations.

8

CLASS OF ONE

By name alone, correspondence courses are uncomplicated: read a textbook or two, answer questions from a course syllabus, test your understanding. Passing the courses means doing this process adequately and consistently. In prison, though, there's more to it because the "classroom" can be a volatile, isolating place where higher learning requires creativity, dedication, and finesse.

Central Prison's library held mostly donated romance, fantasy, suspense, espionage, and true crime novels. The one encyclopedia looked old enough to have been used by junior high schoolers in the 90s. No computer or internet access meant relying on daily *News* and *Observer* newspapers and magazines like *Time* or *National Geographic*, and TV or radio news programs, for any kind of research. Researching topics related to my courses was difficult at best.

If questions about criminal justice theory or symbolic logic could not be answered from the textbook, I could write the professor and hope he or she responded, but this took several weeks through the mail. Courses with a dozen lessons, and a professor who took four to six weeks to return graded lessons, made communicating by mail an arduous process. Doing so with two or three courses wasted precious time. Each course had an eight-month expiration date, and while the university allowed for a four-month extension, spending a year on one course to satisfy my questions would throw off my schedule. Besides, it was expected that independent and distance learning students try to figure things out on their own.

Academic advisors supported this idea. Their responses to questions were never more than a paragraph that encouraged communication with professors. Advisors' advice related to course registration, deadlines, and administrative matters about transfers or transcripts. Part of the reason for this had to do with the Degree Audit Report System (DARS), which promoted independence

DOI: 10.4324/9781003449454-11

and guidelines for course selection. The other part is that advisors have too many students, and are too far removed from incarcerated students, to understand their specific needs. Without access to a phone or email, "guiding" incarcerated students becomes a cursory role for many academic advisors, one often undermined by the stigma of prison.

Asking my parents or friends for help brought mixed results. Sometimes they could provide valuable points that made me reconsider how I viewed a particular subject. When those questions related to nuance with Robert Merton's anomie strain theory, or even federal acts protecting people in the workplace, such things received blank stares. I discovered that, when attempting to explain sociology, my grasp of the subject was not strong enough. I needed the open discussion of a classroom with other students and instructors to refine my understanding. Not having access to that interaction was a disadvantage of independent and distance learning, but one I had to overcome.

Prison is all about disadvantage. Whether one has a release date or not, doing time is about finding relief from the pains and indignities of confinement. Money has a lot to do with achieving relief, but most prisoners are indigent, and earning 40–60 cents a day for prison labor (often 40–60-hour work weeks) that is often degrading does nothing for one's pockets. This makes finessing limited resources an important skill to learn in prison.

"Finesse" is resource strategy—doing as much as possible with little or making something out of nothing. Finesse is about more than money or goods; it is an ability to create comfort and fulfill needs by paying attention to details. This is how wine is made from fruit and candy, "stingers" (heating elements) from discarded wire and scrap metal, and tattoo ink from Styrofoam. However much society desires to rid itself of people in prison, American ingenuity thrives here. "Advantage" in prison is as much about food, safety, and peace as it is freedom from deprivation. In my case, it meant filling the gap where a classroom should have been. In a class of one, higher learning requires a little finesse.

I learned the basic rules of finesse from old man Roper. A loan shark who used to live in the Appalachian Mountains and make moonshine, Roper often said, "Yankee, don't spend money you ain't got." Dying of cancer and emphysema when we met in 1999, Roper heard my Maine accent and immediately dubbed me "Yankee." Unable to read well, Roper asked me and other friends to read westerns to him. The trade-off: usually advice.

"Yankee, you gotta learn to do without in prison. Nobody is gonna hold your hand or tell you it's 'okay.' You're not here for an easy ride, but that don't mean you can't help yourself."

Roper showed me finesse is about perspective. Prison was only the disadvantage I allowed it to be. I did not have to be corrupted by prison norms to "get high," join a gang, succumb to violence at the first opportunity, or vegetate because it's the only path presented. Plenty of people provided much needed guidance and life experiences with important lessons that benefited my pursuit of higher education. Society may have discarded our value as human beings, but I discovered ways to mine it.

Maintaining my own schedule meant completing assignments every other week. In this way, two or three courses could be completed within the eight-month expiration date. But doing so left a few months before registering for and beginning new courses, a necessary break to catch up on some fiction reading and relax. I also took this time to apply many of the things I studied. There were few opportunities to do this, but Dungeons and Dragons (D+D) created that space.

The purest form of imagination and immersive storytelling, D+D consumed time in a way that the uninitiated struggle to understand. At its core, role-playing games (RPGs) like D+D present an opportunity to be a part of a story, create legends, make decisions for characters, and dictate the course of a plot. As a child I enjoyed "Choose Your Own Adventure" novels, which gave readers two or three plot options each chapter, like: "Turn to page 16 if Max uses the iron key" or "Skip to Chapter Three if Gwen crosses the bridge." Instead of one ending, a few became possible. Comparatively, RPGs are exponentially more complex because the characters are controlled by players making real-time decisions with their own knowledge, attitudes, beliefs, and emotions.

RPGs necessitate and develop critical thinking, strategizing, problem solving, creativity, diplomacy, initiative, team building, and leadership skills. Where successful game sessions award characters "experience points" for accomplishing a variety of tasks, failure can mean character death and starting over from scratch. The more one invests time and effort into character development, the more one thinks through a challenge and comes up with inventive solutions. Just like reality, proactive thinking enables players to overcome most obstacles.

Some prisons ban D+D books and gaming materials because of super-stitious fears and the belief they promote too much escapism. This might prevent "official" versions of the game, but not bootleg RPGs, which need only willing players with imaginations. Whether the prison banned or ignored the game hardly mattered to us, though it would have been encouraging to know the California Department of Corrections recognizes RPGs as a reha-bilitative tool. Hawke Robinson, a California Department of Health Regis-tered Therapist, even founded RPG Research and RPG Therapeutics LLC as a reentry program.

Role-playing and life scenarios may be good to prepare prisoners for their return to society, but we largely played for fun. Initially, my decisions mir-rored those of reality; short-sighted, devoid of details, compulsive and reck-less. After taking a dozen college courses, though, my decision making involved greater analysis, logic, awareness, and task orientation. I preferred being a game master (GM), who manages the game, arbitrates the rules, and builds worlds in which player characters lived. As GM, I digested numerous core rule books on game mechanics and character development, immediately recognizing many of the concepts I learned in personality psychology.

D+D was an incubator of creativity where everyone sought to be and do more than the limited world of prison allows. None of us were prisoners in D+D. With infinite resources from the imagination, anything and everything became possible. That was the draw of RPGs and cause of concern from more punitive prison officials: escape from mindless obedience and the power to control the impossible in a place that rendered us seemingly powerless.

As a natural progression of the creative process, I began entering the annual NCDOC writing contest. Each of the three categories—essay, short story, poetry—awarded certificates to five winners. NCDOC programs and rehabilitative service administrators reviewed the entries and determined who won, but did not otherwise compile, publish, disseminate, or reward the writing. I convinced myself that entering a prison writing contest was just practice, but when my entries didn't place, the competition seized my interest. I tried again the following year and placed second with an essay exploring a question I once asked Fr. Dan: if Christ was the embodiment of altruism, did he *really* sacrifice anything? I placed fourth the next year with a short story scene of St. Peter "at the gates," checking the ledger for an obese corporate executive who had been selfish his whole life. My stories had morals and my essays challenged popular assumptions. Sometimes the writing could be good, mostly it was rudimentary.

In 2011, I enrolled in four courses to see if I could handle the heavier workload, and shave off the number of years it would take to complete the associate degree. It was not lost on me that completing two or three courses each year failed to equal a full college load. It was the first time I enrolled in courses without lessons. Course credit by examination (CCE) cut the completion time in half because no mailed lessons or mid-terms were required. Read a textbook, take a comprehensive three-hour exam. There was more pressure to succeed, but my confidence and competence had grown.

I took two CCE courses—*Abnormal Psychology* and *Developmental Psychology*—and two courses with lessons—*Astronomy* and *Nutrition*. *Abnormal Psychology* taught me a lot about recognizing and diagnosing mental illness. Naturally, I turned my sights inward, but found equally interesting, weird, and sad examples around me. High numbers of depression, OCD and other anxiety-based disorders, schizophrenia, but fewer sociopaths than the public has been led to believe by criminologists. A high rate of learning disabilities and plenty of people with multiple illnesses that went undiagnosed or untreated. Not that treatment amounted to much more than heavy doses of psychotropic medications and solitary confinement. Even as the textbooks illustrated symptoms, genetic predispositions, developmental milestones, and a plethora of research and experiments, I began to better understand my adolescence. Where counseling and rehab failed to help develop skills necessary to improving my mental health, studying psychology, and an overwhelming desire to change helped meet that need. Yet, while independent learning often meant solving my own problems, and resourcefulness allowed me to squeeze water from the stones of my prison, both have their limits.

Near the end of my associate degree's required credits, I took several business courses as electives because doing so seemed practical. I also wanted a change of pace from studying psychology and sociology. As it turned out, *Small Business Operations, Elements of Supervision*, and *Business Report Writing* contained avenues to main themes of subjects I already studied. This was especially true of the techniques taught in *Business Report Writing* and the dissection of bureaucracy in *Elements of Supervision*. After acing all three, and needing only three more courses to finish the AA, I enrolled in *Critical Approaches to Drama, Punishment in Society*, and *Business Law*.

These three courses were a finish line I never imagined reaching. It had taken nearly eight plodding years, but the end was in sight.

Business law is nothing like criminal law. Nor was it like any social science or business course I took. The course level may have designated it as 255 (sophomore level, thus, less difficult than junior or senior), but this was misleading. Not all textbooks are easy to understand. Some, like *Elements of Supervision*, are interesting to read, easy to absorb, and organized clearly. Other textbooks, like *Introduction to Philosophy*, are unclear and extremely dense. The *Business Law* textbook was the size of an unabridged dictionary and just as exciting to read. Antitrust laws, contracts, agency, real estate, litigation, fiduciary duty—these and other concepts made my head spin. All of it was technical, convoluted, and boring. For the first time I regretted enrolling in *Business Law* as a CCE course.

Because most of the *Business Law* concepts were new, I struggled to retain them. I read each chapter, read it again while taking notes and highlighting key terms, answered questions at the end of each chapter, and reviewed my notes. I had no memorization techniques, instead relying on familiarity with the subject. Each chapter also included U.S. Supreme Court rulings related to important precedent-setting legal procedure. I read these but struggled to comprehend their significance beyond illustrative examples. There was no one to ask for help—it was my responsibility to know.

The *Business Law* CCE exam consisted of multiple choice, short answer, definition questions, and essay questions. When the exam began, all my niggling concerns became a trickle of fear. The material appeared foreign, as if the exam covered a different textbook. The confusion was all mine, though. I found myself guessing, leaving questions blank and feeling like a fraud. What the hell was promissory estoppel? Why the hell did I choose *Business Law*?

The ensuing F on the course report should not have surprised me. I failed by one percentage point. Desperate and unwilling to give up, I wrote and asked the professor to review the exam and see if he overlooked a percentage point.

He responded with an angry retort on my letter and stapled it to the grade report. "I certainly will not review your exam. Students who study, pass. Students who don't fail."

Failure is a curdling, sick feeling in the pit of the stomach. It turns skin clammy, prickles scalps, tastes bitter, and made me want to hide under a rock. Failure is the sound of derisive laughter, a guard dismissing you as nothing more than an inmate, and a cell door slamming shut. Carelessness, over-confidence that hid incompetence, and a lack of guidance led to my *Business Law* failure. I appealed the grade to the assistant dean of Ohio University, something my advisor suggested after-the-fact (instead of "Hey, maybe you shouldn't enroll in a CCE course outside of your major"). Nothing came of the appeal, not even a response.

My parents always encouraged their children. At no time did Mom or Dad say, "You can't accomplish that" or "You're not good enough." They pushed us and said, "Try," "Practice," and "Do it until you succeed." If we did poorly or failed, they said, "Try harder" or asked, "What can you do differently?" As a teen, rather than bounce back and learn from my mistakes, I quit. Giving up was easier. That type of thinking is common in prison, especially amongst those who come from dysfunctional households and have no incentive to change. As an adult striving to do and be more than my failures in the free world, quitting is unacceptable. I had come too far, accomplished too much, to let the *Business Law* failure derail my journey. In a class of one, success requires tenacity.

9

ASSOCIATE DEGREE

One of the most hated rituals in prison is standing in line for chow. With an average wait time of 15–20 minutes three times a day, seven days a week, lining up for a tray is a mind-numbing aspect of incarceration. Years of confinement threaded with thousands of hours standing around while inane and vitriolic conversations drone, impatience shuffles the feet and fantasies of the latest Olive Garden special sour when whatever unidentified concoction is slopped on a tray and shoved out the serving window.

While standing in line for supper one June evening in 2013, the assistant unit manager walked up to me waving a folded piece of paper.

"Lyle May? Lyle May! I've got something you want."

She narrowed her eyes at the snickers and lewd comments from other prisoners standing in line. Not expecting any paperwork like a response from a grievance, I assumed it to be a weekly trust fund update given to every prisoner whether they have made money or not. I put it in my pocket.

"Aren't you gonna open it?" She smiled. "Careful when you do."
Frowning at the attention, I removed the staple and unfolded the paper.

The Board of Trustees of
The Ohio University
On the recommendation of the faculty in recognition of the completion of
the prescribed course in the
University College
has conferred upon
Lyle C. May
The degree of

DOI: 10.4324/9781003449454-12

Associate in Arts
With all the honors, rights, and privileges belonging thereto.
In witness thereof this diploma has been signed by the duly authorized
Office of the university and the Board of Trustees and sealed with its
corporate seal.
Given the two hundred ninth year of the University
at Athens, Ohio, on May fourth, two thousand fourteen.

I smoothed out the folds, staring at the diploma seal and signatories.
A flash of irritation. "Why can't I have the original?"

'The assistant unit manager rolled her eyes, hand on hips, and spoke as if to a child or dog in a mocking high-pitched voice. "Why can't I have the original? Because you can't have documents like that. Jeez. Thank me and be glad I gave you a photocopy."

It had been nearly nine years since my first letter to Mr. Mac asking permission to enroll in a college course. Though my interactions with staff were limited and always polite to avoid problems, sometimes anger surfaced, and I had to grit my teeth to keep it in. Whatever had to be done. In a place where only two prison administrators supported my higher education, diplomacy was a must. One complaint or query or vindictive staff member who disliked the idea of a death row prisoner having access to college could end it instantly.

"Thank you." I said, picking up my tray to go sit with friends.

Back on the block, I laminated the diploma with clear packing tape and put a cardboard back on it. I taped it to the wall of my cell. Days passed before I looked at the diploma, unsure what to think. The document represented the completion of 20 college courses, thousands of hours of studying over two dozen textbooks, thousands of pages of written notes, and dozens of exams. My time had been invested rather than squandered to reach the only significant accomplishment of my life. The original copy of the diploma went to my parents; something to temper the pain of my countless failures. Here, at last, was proof that potential for growth remained. But what did it mean for the future?

In the seven years since a de-facto moratorium halted executions, little changed on death row. The state's death penalty shifted into legal limbo as an increasing number of prisoners received life without parole at capital trials or after successful post-conviction appeals. Several people even had their sentence and conviction vacated and were released from prison for a lack of evidence, signaling potential innocence. Then, a legal battle over the Racial Justice Act ensued. The 2009 law, passed by a democrat-controlled North Carolina General Assembly, intended to redress systematic racism in capital punishment. But Republicans saw it as a way to end the death penalty, and when they regained a supermajority in the General Assembly, repealed the law in 2013, but not before over 135 death row prisoners filed claims under the law. The litigation unofficially suspended most capital appeals as attorneys and prosecutors and judges awaited the State Supreme Court's decision. Death sentences stretched into uncertain life sentences with only a remote possibility of execution.

My legal position remained vague. Though I was contesting my conviction and sentence it guaranteed nothing. I clung to hope of relief like a man adrift at sea, believing rescue could come, but knowing appellate relief didn't necessarily mean release. It could still mean death by incarceration. Except, earning an associate degree bolstered my hopes. What you do in prison matters. Judges, prosecutors, parole commissions, clemency boards, and even appellate attorneys look at a defendant's prison record when considering sentencing reductions. Whether explicit or implicit, they all have the same questions. Is this person worth saving? Has he or she changed? Can they contribute to society? Very few criminal justice representatives who oversee "second look mechanisms" will help a prisoner unless he or she demonstrates a willingness to help themselves. As unpredictable as the future is, it behooved me to show others my value as a human being and productive member of society.

As a rehabilitative measure, the associate degree meant adhering to the highest standard of behavior. The state expected me to silently rot and die. Few people who think of death row prisoners, if they think of us at all, expect anything positive or life changing. By earning a degree though, I defied stereotypes and ordinary expectations, proving that with time and resources intellectual advancement in prison—rehabilitation—is possible. My achievement strikes at the heart of the tough-on-crime retributive model of criminal justice. "Lock 'em up and throw the key away" is a penal philosophy that does not necessarily improve public safety and ignores fundamental truth about human beings in confinement: people adapt and learn if given half a chance and the right motivation.

I felt no puffed-up sense of pride when looking at the diploma taped to my wall. Only responsibility. To do more and be more now that it was obvious I had the potential.

One friend asked, "What's wrong with you? I'd be satisfied having gotten that far, tellin' everybody and their mamas I earned a degree. You done more than anyone else on the row and a lot of guys in prison. Be happy."

Doing good for someone in prison, not as a student or 35-year-old man, rankled. Earning a degree became a complex examination of my future, identity, goals, and expectations. There were no more blue prints unless I looked to historical figures. No one on death row could advise me going forward. To my friends I reached the pinnacle and now they cheered me on. To my parents I fulfilled long-held beliefs about my potential. Outside of the people who genuinely cared about me, I had merely shown that any monkey with a typewriter and enough time can compose Shakespeare.

Or, as one sergeant said to a couple of new officers when they saw me sign for some course materials, "May's okay, he's a smart inmate."

Prison standards and expectations would never satisfy me. Earning an associate degree shrank on the scale of achievement to a goal that should have been reached two years after graduating high school. While choosing higher education as an adult in prison had been a life-changing decision, and earning a degree is great by any measure, my bar has been raised.

I began writing the memoir *Waiting for the Last Train* while waiting for my course materials to arrive. My mom suggested writing about my childhood memories and experiences as a teen. The challenge of writing a book appealed to me, I had entered a number of short stories and essays to the annual NCDOC writing contest with varying degrees of success, but writing an autobiography was altogether different. Deeper, personal, reflective, and at times cathartic, exorcising long-held sectors of childhood and adolescence helped me leave the past behind while learning from it. I grieved as I wrote, tapping into emotions smothered by drugs, alcohol and willful ignorance. Writing *Waiting for the Last Train* became a form of therapy without the creepy stranger or calculating institutional staffer digging through the detritus of my life. I wrote to find the Lyle who had fallen between the cracks even as I applied simple things gleaned from psychology.

Though doing the hard work of critical self-reflection helped me mature, my writing lacked illustration of that trek. I gathered moments in my life that stuck out, trying to recreate a chronological narrative of events only to discover they lacked development and perspective. None of my college English teachers—there were six—discussed the nature of soliloquies in narrative nonfiction or how to carry out that story over numerous chapters. Nevertheless, a lack of experience didn't stop me. I completed a decent fourth draft of the book and, with the help of some friends and my dad, had it typed up and self-published on Amazon eBooks for Kindle.

While writing the book I thought about my next courses. At the time, my academic advisor provided no guidance. To be honest, I hadn't expected to live long enough to finish the associate degree. But that sort of fatalism could no longer be supported by evidence of the moment or my evolving worldview. Ohio University's Correctional Education Program offered a Bachelor of Specialized Studies degree, but that was a long-term goal. It took nearly nine years to earn an associate degree: did I have another nine years of patience, diligence, and determination? Would my sponsor fund another 20 courses? I knew more courses were in my immediate future, but how would they connect with a bachelor's degree?

When my friend Chief heard I was taking college courses he urged me to study the law.

"Cuz, whatever you do you need to learn about the law. You can't always depend on these lawyers to tell you everything. You gonna sit here and let some stranger who doesn't care about you spendin' the rest of your life in prison determine your fate? Who are you to them other than a paycheck? Study the law, cuz. Keep em' honest. They don't owe you nothin', but you owe yourself everything."

The conversation went on in that vein, at times bitter and cynical, but nonetheless true. Living through so many executions, many of them friends who believed their attorneys would save them, made it difficult to trust lawyers. Some people simply couldn't be saved. Others dropped their appeals in a state-assisted suicide. However, enough evidence existed among the living to prove legal representation for capital defendants does not mean "adequate" or "effective" representation. Many prisoners hadn't heard from their attorneys in years. Sometimes filing deadlines were missed. I didn't want to be the guy who had access to an education and failed to learn enough to hold his lawyers accountable. Since North Carolina's prisons do not have law libraries, this is especially difficult. Fortunately, as if an answer to my need, Ohio University began offering a Paralegal Certificate Program through the Center for Legal Studies in Golden, Colorado.

The Paralegal Certificate Program taught the basics about the legal system in a two-part course. Between the paralegal text, legal dictionary, Federal Civil Procedure Handbook, The Bluebook of Citations, and photocopied reports explaining Shepherdization and writing an appellate brief, I quickly learned how much legal research and development paralegals do for lawyers. Some of the concepts were slightly familiar. You don't sit through a capital trial, lose a direct appeal, read through trial transcripts and other documents, and live around people with the same experiences and fail to pick up some legal terminology. At a minimum I better understood the structure of the criminal legal system and its reliance on precedent or "stare decisis." It helped not to be completely ignorant of how the state and court work, but it also empowered me in some small yet important ways.

After completing the paralegal certificate, I grew interested enough in the field to inquire about what it took to become a certified paralegal. I wrote to the North Carolina State Bar Association. When the Bar's response came back, it explained that paralegals have a bachelor's degree, often in criminology or paralegalism, and a number of CLE courses required for certification and hiring purposes. The letter went on to state the Bar does not recognize "paralegal certificates" and kindly thanked me for my interest. It was an embarrassing moment that made me feel foolish for thinking it would be easy.

I grew discouraged. Had I taken a wrong turn? Doubt about the authenticity of my education crept into my thoughts. A lack of communication and guidance from academic advisors left me guessing which courses to take. The degree audit report gave only a general outline and while I had enrolled in correspondence courses this did not mean that I was registered for the BSS degree program. I did not know that at the time though. Uncertainty, doubt, endless obstacles, and my inability to understand how best to direct my degree became bricks in a wall that suddenly appeared ready to end my pursuit of higher education.

A tiny part of me wanted to quit. I had done enough. My standards were unreasonable. Giving up would be easier than pushing past the exhaustion, easier than trying, easier than dealing with constant impediments to college in prison. Thankfully, that weak mindset that had dominated my adolescence no longer held any power. It could not compete with the world of opportunity and critical thinking. It was okay to be tired. It would never be okay to quit.

The associate degree taped to the wall of my cell is a symbol of defiance, a candle flame pushing back the darkness of ignorance, guttering at times, but burning brightly. Old ideas that made doing nothing and being nothing seem acceptable have been replaced with perspective, intelligence, determination, hope, faith, and the courage to reach beyond walls. Driving this transformative journey is the belief that in the singular act of trying to learn I succeed. Where it leads, whatever the challenges and frustrations, it's my duty to complete the journey. I owe myself that and more.

References

Arjini, N. K., Berstain, M. M., & Karabel, S. A. (2018, March 25). Beyond bars, beyond gates. *The Harvard Crimson*. www.thecrimson.com/article/2018/3/5/arjini-bernstein-karabel-beyond-bars/.

Bartollas, C., & Schmalleger, F. (2014). *Juvenile Delinquency* (9th ed.). Pearson.

Butterfield, F. (2004, May 8). Mistreatment of prisoners is called routine in U.S. *The New York Times*.

Gottschalk, M. (2015). *Caught: The Prison State and the Lockdown of American Politics*. Princeton University Press.

Gibney, B. C. (2019). *The Nonsense Factory: The Making and Breaking of the American Legal System*. Hatchell Books.

Hassine, V. (2011) *Life Without Parole: Living and Dying in Prison Today* (5th ed.). Oxford University Press.

Herbert, B. (2004, May 31). America's Abu Ghraib. *The New York Times*.

Hurley, M. H. (2018). *Aging in Prison: The Integration of Research and Practice* (2nd ed.). Carolina Academic Press.

Johnson, R., Rocheleau, A. M., & Martin, A. B. (2017). *Hard Time* (4th ed.). Wiley-Blackwell.

Louisiana sheriff cages suicidal prisoners in space smaller than required for dogs. (2011, June 15). *Prisons Legal News*, 18. www.prisonlegalnews.org/news/2011/jun/15/louisiana-sheriff-cages-suicidal-prisoners-in-space-smaller-than-required-for-dogs/.

Tucker, J. B. (2009). *The Liberal Arts Unbound: Higher Education in an American Prison, 2005–2006*. [Doctoral dissertation, Columbia University]. Proquest. http://search.proquest.com/docview/304862310.

Visher, C. A. (2007). Returning home: Emerging findings and policy lessons about prisoner reentry. *Federal Sentencing Reporter*, 20(2), 93–102.

Worth, R. (1995, November). A model prison. *The Atlantic*. www.theatlantic.com/past/docs/issues/95nov/prisons.

PART 4

Convict Criminology, Penal Populism, and why Restoring the Rehabilitative Ideal in Prison is not as Simple as the Return of Pell Grant Access

Convict criminology arose from a lack of perspective by orthodox criminologists' analysis of prisons. Particularly, there has been a dearth of research and analysis of prison systems, conditions, culture, and dysfunction. Typically, orthodox criminologists research prisons from the outside in an attempt to be objective, but this position fails to uncover important details of the carceral experience, and the recommendations for penal and sentencing policy are necessarily flawed. In contrast, convict criminologists have an insider's knowledge of the carceral experience and are more likely to understand and convey research findings about contributing factors to recidivism, penal failure, and mass incarceration (Ross & Richards, 2003). Convict criminologists do not have exclusive authority on the subject of incarceration, but their experiences of imprisonment provide valuable insight into the closed world of prison and sometimes indecipherable statistics that create criminal legal policy. For the convict criminologist, the lived carceral experience is an advantage in their scholarship (Newbold et al., 2014).

An early progenitor of convict criminology, John Irvin, relied on his intimate knowledge of prison culture to glean valuable information ordinarily lost to or ignored by other criminologists. Irvin challenged orthodox thinking about prison culture and pursued a more humanitarian approach to corrections. He also attacked what he saw as American's "imprisonment binge" policies in the early 1980s (as cited by Newbold et al., 2014, p. 442). It would not be until 1997, in a special session of the American Society of Criminology (ASC) annual conference, that formerly incarcerated academics Chuck Terry,

DOI: 10.4324/9781003449454-13

Rick Jones, Steve Richards, and Ed Tromhauser (with help from Irvin) formally introduced carceral experience into the study of crime, punishment, and corrections (Newbold et al., 2014).

A diverse group with varied experiences, convict criminologists are not uniform in the expression of the carceral lives (Newbold et al., 2014). However, they have all lived and worked with the impact sentencing and correctional policy, causes of penal violence, antagonistic relationships between the incarcerated and correctional staff, and how rehabilitative programs such as higher education fit into this picture (Leyva & Bickel, 2010). Debates among convict criminologists usually revolve around correctional policy applications, research orientation, terminology, and subjective methodology. This might in large part be because prisons are like lifeforms—every facility is different, as is every penal system. Ultimately, convict criminologists can convey the importance of these differences and unite over the belief that carceral experience is a critical element of criminology (Newbold et al., 2014).

At the root of convict criminology is critical criminology, which involves challenging, critiquing, and analyzing every facet of crime, punishment, and corrections. Critical criminology seeks to dispel myths and misconceptions propagated by public officials and mainstream media outlets, demystifying causes of crime, responses by law enforcement, conclusions in the criminal legal system, and outcomes in correctional intervention while offering alternative interpretations and solutions (Ross & Richards, 2003). While critical criminology has anarchist and Marxist influences, convict criminology is less about standing up to "the establishment" and more about bringing nuanced sociological and psychological understanding to penal history, politics, policies, and experience while challenging the false morality imposed by classic criminology. In his book *Crime and Community* (1938), Frank Tannenbaum advances a sociological criminology concerned with meaning and power, providing a view of people within the context of how they respond to life's problems, which arise from social structures not always of their own making (Mooney, 2020). Tannenbaum (1938) believed that criminological discourse too often focused on the differences between the nature of the criminal and non-criminal. This categorization and identification misses the human experience within unequal social stratification by major power holders.

The struggle in defining understanding of crime, punishment, and corrections is best explained by conflict theory. Becker (1963) held that "moral entrepreneurs" find cause for new rules to help gain power, then push for creation of these new rules. Moral entrepreneurs are typically majority power holders. Conflict theory lends important understanding to criminology by explaining evolving definitions of deviance and crime (Frailing & Harper, 2009). Ordinarily, criminologists study crime as observers who frame rules based on research and statistics, colored with their background (typically white, male, middle-class academics), to define deviance. People caught within the nexus of the criminal legal system are more likely to rationalize their behavior as situation-specific and challenge the majority power holders' definitions as inaccurate. While both definitions may carry elements of truth, conflict theory elucidates the tension between conflict and orthodox criminological perspectives just as it would the influence of intersectionality.

Conflict theory posits that laws and their subsequent violation result from a competition for resources, with more powerful actors defining the law and controlling access to resources especially as it relates to economic mobility and education. Maintaining the law and control of resources is in the interest of majority power holders. Minority power holders are likely to be labeled radical, deviant, or "less than" and be accused of violating the law when they pursue resources through systems not made for their benefit (Frailing & Harper, 2009).

With regard to diversification in criminology, conflict theorist August Turk (1969) holds that the relative "organization" and "sophistication" of authorities and subjects influence the likelihood of conflict between them. Authorities are organized and systematic, a prerequisite for achieving and retaining power, but they are also sophisticated, which is the knowledge of others' resource needs and behavioral patterns—enough to be used in manipulation of them (Turk, 1969).

Politicians and other public officials—district attorneys, judges, sheriffs— often seek to maintain office by using high-profile crimes and calling for severe punishment to gain political advantage. They pander to public anxiety over safety then advocate for retributionist policies that do not reduce crime (Roberts et al., 2003). These elected officials largely borrow theoretical constructs from the classical school of criminology: the rationality of crime, utilitarianism, and just deserts. The rationality of crime holds that the person who commits a crime has free will and chooses to violate the law (Fagan & Piquero, 2007). This is an extension of the felicific calculus and deterrence doctrine, namely, that if a person makes a risk-benefit analysis of a criminal act, certain, swift, and severe punishment is more likely to deter the criminal act. Punishment is justified as a utilitarian cause for public safety and the dominant theme is deterrence. "Just deserts" is the belief that people who violate the law "deserve" to be punished severely yet proportionately so the punishment "fits" the crime (Bartollas & Schmalleger, 2014).

Maybe if the classic constructs were not twisted with strains of vengeful retaliation and the puritanical expiation of sin, or people who commit crimes always did so from a rational frame of mind, a classic approach to crime might be logical. Except, there is no historical evidence severe punishments deter crime. There is evidence extreme punishment generates greater levels of hostility in a population, risking the stability of current social order (Mooney, 2020). The causes of crime are also diverse and not always rational, especially amongst the mentally ill and people under 25 years of age who lack full developmental maturity. The tough-on-crime populism of the 1980s and 1990s did not care about evidence or logic. It also represented the belief system of the majority power-holding group. Cost-effective, crime-reducing common sense social reforms that provided safe alternatives to retributivist policies were denigrated as "soft," "liberal," or criminogenic, despite evidence to the contrary. A classic example was used by George H. W. Bush against the governor of Massachusetts, Michael Dukakis, in a 1988 presidential campaign attack ad.

At the time, Massachusetts had a furlough program with a 99% success rate at preventing recidivism among participants (Barkow, 2019). Bush seized on reporting of a violent crime committed by one furloughed person, Willie Horton, and created a political ad that generalized Horton's crime to a risk posed by any prisoner not dealt with harshly. The ad stoked prejudices against African Americans and fear of violent crimes committed by people released by a "soft" criminal legal system. After Dukakis ended the furlough program and lost the race, the "Willie Horton effect" would go on to be used in political campaigns around the country, undermining reasonable and effective early-release mechanisms with fear-mongering devoid of criminological evidence (Kappeler & Potter, 2018).

Fearmongering largely drove arguments that ended incarcerated individuals' Pell Grant eligibility in 1994. Except that, senators mixed in class-based appeals of privilege and limited resources during an economic recession:

> We've got to stop giving a free college education to prison inmates, or else the people who cannot afford to go to college are going to start committing crimes so they can get sent to prison to get a free education … you tell them [middle-class families] that, if their son or daughter committed a violent felony, they would be eligible for a free education, their eyes fall out of their head—Governor of Massachusetts, William Weld [R], 1991.
>
> *(Page, 2004, p. 358)*

> … we will soon have the best educated prison population in the world—but we will have sacrificed the hopes and dreams of hundreds of thousands of young men and women, who have always been good citizens … who have always done what society expected of them … who earned a chance to further their education and better their lives—Texas Senator Kay Bailey Hutchison [R], 1993.
>
> *(Page, 2004, p. 364)*

> You may teach inmates how to fix automobiles, you may teach them how to write, certainly how to read—and the Federal Government funds such programs—but a college education free of charge? No, sir.—North Carolina Senator Jesse Helms [R], 1991
>
> *(Page, 2004, p. 365).*

Facts did not matter to these elected officials and others who voted for the 1994 Omnibus Crime Bill. Eligible citizens were never denied access to Pell Grants because, as a quasi-entitlement, the money came from a pool set aside for low- or no-income individuals (Feeley & Simon, 1992). Moreover, "rewarding" incarcerated people with the opportunity to earn their way out of prison and poverty ignores the hard work it takes to achieve a degree. Attaining a higher education is a rewarding journey, but lawmakers and populists conflate the process with access, maybe on purpose. These myth makers refuse to acknowledge better decision making and economic stability are critical to successful reentry by formerly incarcerated people. If one wanted to limit access to the middle-class and control related resources, they need only claim the most important resource—higher education—is a "privilege" restricted to those who are thought to be "worthy." Though some lawmakers fought against this classism as was indicated by the minority who supported maintenance of Pell Grant access for incarcerated people.

After the passage of the 1994 Omnibus Crime Bill, penal populism was ascendant, militarizing prison guards, returning to chain gangs and convict leasing, and closing the gate on second chances. The devaluation of the incarcerated made it easier to ignore mass incarceration and its disproportionate impact on BIPOC communities. While many criminal justice practitioners—judges, attorneys, and prison officials—tried to resist and remained committed to the rehabilitative ideal, most politicians and penologists now defined penal success in terms of correctional management (Feeley & Simon, 1992). However, the lack of rehabilitative programs and incentives left a void filled by gangs, which in turn made prisons more dangerous, violent, and difficult to manage (Johnson et al., 2017).

Criminologists identify policymaking from emotional public responses to government myth making as "penal populism" (Pratt, 2007). Based in anti-intellectualism, penal populists feed on public mistrust of correctional experts' ability to prevent recidivism. Once the media displays sensational crimes and television shows that glorify law enforcement, prisoners are labeled as "the bad guy" or "monsters," largely unredeemable, opportunistic, untrustworthy, immoral, and "less than" in a way that ignores the human dignity of incarcerated people. One of the most damaging facets of penal populism is that lawmakers suggested any criminal justice practitioner who supported higher education and Pell Grant eligibility for the incarcerated was no better than a criminal (Page, 2004). This rhetoric continues to impact the penal landscape today.

As time went, the U.S. continued to imprison more citizens per capita than any other nation in the world. In an attempt to adjust course and address recidivism, Congress passed the bipartisan 2008 Second Chance Act to provide some funding for prison education and rehabilitation—about $50 per prisoner (Gibney, 2019). Even some conservative and populist lawmakers would likely privately acknowledge the country cannot incarcerate its way out of crime, but they lack the political will or interest to address the causes of mass incarceration or the flow of the school-to-prison pipeline.

In 2015, the U.S. Department of Education announced the Second Chance Pell Grant Experimental Sites Initiative, which began with 65 colleges providing PSCE programs at nearby prisons (Pettit, 2019). Over the next five years, Second Chance Pell enabled 130 colleges in 42 states to serve up to 12,000 incarcerated students annually, providing certificate and degree programs, but it was a small percentage of those who needed access (Chestnut & Wachendorfer, 2021).

Lawmakers discussed lifting the ban on Pell Grants for the incarcerated in the years following the Second Chance Pell, but there was still significant resistance in the Republican party (Krieghbaum, 2019). Despite the opposition, on December 27, 2020, Congress passed a $1.4 trillion omnibus spending bill that, amongst other items, included the FASFA (Free Application for Student Aid) Simplification Act.

The FAFSA Simplification Act (2021) reversed the ban on Pell Grant eligibility for people confined in prisons, jails, and civil commitment facilities throughout the U.S. and its territories. The law will take effect no later than July 1, 2023, and is the first time since the early 1990s that every incarcerated person has access to federal funding for PSCE programs (Martinez-Hill, 2021). Considering the political penal drama behind Pell Grant eligibility, there is cause to celebrate the FAFSA Simplification Act (2021) because it is "sentence-blind," which makes over 2 million incarcerated people eligible for PSCE funding. It almost sounds too good to be true.

What has originally been touted as a "sentence-blind" law comes with a provision that grants ultimate authority over PSCE programs to state and federal corrections leaders. In other words, a director or commissioner of a state's penal system, a position typically filled by executive branch appointment, will determine which colleges provide courses to the incarcerated, what degree or certificate programs are available, and who may participate (FAFSA Simplification Act, 2021).

Since passage of the FAFSA Simplification Act, the U.S. Department of Education has held committee meetings about implementation of the law. Prison Education subcommittee members have voiced concern about giving prison officials control over access to Pell funded PSCE programs (West, 2021). "The DOC is not an educational institution, yet they are able to make all of the education decisions"—Terrence S. McTier, Director, Prison Education Project, Washington University (West, 2021, p. 2).

Senior policy analyst for Higher Education at American Progress, Bradley Custer claimed that a prison system cannot be forced to approve a PSCE program, suggesting that the onus of implementing college in prison programs is the responsibility of colleges (West, 2021). Seeking clarification, Open Campus Media posed the question of control and access directly to the U.S. Department of Education at one of their January 2022 subcommittee meetings:

Q. OPEN CAMPUS MEDIA: The FASFA Simplification Act states that students must be enrolled in or accepted to a qualifying prison education program, but the law is "sentence-blind," meaning that all incarcerated people are eligible, regardless of conviction or sentence length. Does this prevent states or individual prisons from blocking eligibility?

A. U.S. DEPARTMENT OF EDUCATION: The FASFA Simplification Act speaks to Pell Grant access. While a school or correctional system can continue to determine who may enroll in a program, if an individual is enrolled in an eligible prison education program, a school or correctional system would not be allowed to block them from accessing Pell Grants if they otherwise qualify under federal rules.

The purpose of convict criminology is to shine a light on the dark corners of the penal system and lend greater perspective to criminology as a field. Through their experience and scholarship, convict criminologists challenge orthodox thinking about corrections. Orthodox criminologists likely believe the FAFSA Simplification Act is a panacea for rehabilitative programing. Convict criminologists know better. Everyone in prison likely knows better. The nature of modern U.S. prisons will resist an injection of rehabilitative programs. Certain prisons will host pockets of resistance to penal populism as they always have. The penal populists amongst prison officials are likely to restrict PSCE access. Barriers in the form of bureaucratic stalling will frustrate some prisoners so much that it may deter them from participating in PSCE programming. Higher education in prison is by no means an easy path; it is quite the opposite.

Without federal oversight of access to Pell-funded programs and fierce activism by local colleges on behalf of everyone in prison, prison officials will do as they have always done—whatever they want. This status quo is, of course, unacceptable. The fight for access to higher education did not end with the FAFSA Simplification Act. Penal populism did not disappear beneath the gaze of an awakened nation. It remains the mortar of mass incarceration. Conflict is imperative if that mortar is to be dissolved.

In a healthy democracy, safety depends on effective, evidence-based decisions by criminal justice practitioners, the voting public, lawmakers, and the incarcerated. The path to public safety must be trod with higher education. We know what happens when anti-intellectualists win; it is past time to return them to the annals of history and put an end to penal populism.

10

PROGRAMS

One day in August 2013, a memo appeared on every cell block bulletin board of death row. Such notices normally restricted some aspects of our highly constrained life and made it harder. This memo did not. *Writing From Captivity* advertised the opportunity for participants to read and discuss essays and books written by historical figures in confinement. Only 20 people would be selected for the group. Interested parties could submit a letter to Dr. K, director of Psychological Services at Central Prison.

The memo drew people to the bulletin board as they speculated on hidden meanings, conspiracies, and whether it was some kind of trick. Ordinarily, the Recreation Department hosted the only "programs" other than religious services: fast food sales that funded recreational equipment and movies, and an annual basketball tournament. While the Division of Prisons hosted annual art and writing contests, *Writing From Captivity* appeared to be different.

Central Prison had not offered educational programs to death row since the early 1990s, before the end of prisoners' access to Federal Pell Grants that funded college programs. Since then, the Programs Department did little for the general prison population and even less for death row. At one time, case managers doubled as social workers, ensuring prisoners met the appropriate criterion for parole, but that was before the North Carolina General Assembly abolished parole in 1994. Since then, case managers became little more than extensions of custody staff who assigned jobs, filed interprison transfers, and moonlighted as members of the FCC, a board that reviews cases of prisoners in disciplinary segregation, rubber-stamping stays in solitary confinement that could last years.

Most prisoners were dismissive of, or derided, the Programs Department because the name was empty of meaning. Even though Policy and Procedures explicitly stated numerous leisure structured, special, and recognition activities

DOI: 10.4324/9781003449454-14

that should have been provided to the prison population, the Associate Warden of Programs (AWOP) did not carry out that policy. Prisoners had no recourse because most wardens were security-minded; rehabilitation was a perk to them. Even individual activities like arts and crafts were denied simply because prison officials refused to enforce their own policies.

As a result, Central Prison became a processing hub through which prisoners transferred to other facilities, stayed in the general population unit, or were confined on one of the high-security units like Death Row, Mental Health, and Unit One (solitary confinement). That penal administrators and wardens were okay with this warehousing spoke volumes.

Then came Dr. K at the head of mental health reforms throughout the state prison system. New Mental Health Policy and Procedure, based on research and applications in other state prison systems, minimized the use of psychotropic medications to treat mental illnesses and maximized prevention of symptoms through "Active Treatment Components," which included, but was not limited to:

(A) Activities to enhance social skills and reduce isolation
(B) Recreational activities
(C) Literacy activities
(D) Core Therapy such as: Psychological Education, Anger Management, Relaxation, Fitness, Life Management, Depression Management, Music, Self-Care Skills, Transitions/Release Planning, Horticulture Therapy, Accepting Responsibility, and Social Anxiety
(E) Leisure Skills
(F) Special Events—May include activities such as birthday parties, bingo, or recognition of achievement ceremonies
(G) Elective Choice activities including Interpersonal Coping Strategies, Current Events, Natural Sciences, Crafts, Advanced Art, and Reading as well as other Core activities.
(H) Horticulture—Involving plant propagation, maintenance, and vegetable gardening

> *(Health Services Policy and Procedure Manual; Section: Core and Treatment of Patient—Adult Residential Treatment Services; Policy #TX I-14, Page 7 of 10).*

The Active Treatment Components did everything the Programs Department should have been doing, but with the weight of legislative support behind it and increased attention on the mental health of prisoners. Though we did not know it at the time, *Writing From Captivity* was an attempt to implement these policies on a unit in which nearly half the prisons (about 65) consumed psychotropic medications. This enabled Dr. K to do on death row what the Programs Department would not.

Fifty people sent letters of interest for *Writing From Captivity*. I sent one because the idea of a writing group intrigued me and it would be good practice. When the group of 20 convened, we sat in a large circle of chairs in Unit-Three's multi-purpose room, an empty concrete room usually reserved for religious services. Dr. K, a tall lanky ginger-haired man in his 40s, stood in the center, smiling.

"Welcome to *Writing From Captivity*," he said. "I'm so glad you've chosen to participate. The fact is you guys need something to stimulate and expand your thinking. So, we're going to learn what it means to write from a place of confinement. How previous writers have expressed that experience." He grinned, hands clasped in front of him as if ready to bow, looking excited. "We're going to do some of our own writing too. First, I want to go around and have everyone introduce themselves. Say your name and something you like to do, a favorite sports team."

Isaac, a Mennonite Minister and volunteer, helped Dr. K teach the class. They gave us notebooks, pens, and photocopied handouts of chapters from classic literature. Despite the lack of grades and tests, *Writing From Captivity* felt much like an ordinary class with lectures, discussions, homework assignments, and the expectation everyone would try his hardest.

The lack of judgment on ability and genuine interest in every participant enabled enjoyment of the topics. Once basic ground rules for discussion and criticism had been established, every class ended too quickly, with some conversation continuing into the following week. Even when it became obvious a number of people lacked a general grasp of grammar and two struggled to read, rather than turn it into an English class, Isaac gave some pointers and kept things moving along.

None of us had been in a classroom in a very long time. I found it hard to voice my opinion, mouth drying, sweaty hands shaking, and thoughts scattering like frightened pigeons. Despite knowing and growing up around most of the guys in the class it didn't suddenly make me confident, comfortable, or well-spoken. For the entire nine years my higher education had been conducted in the seclusion of a cell. I couldn't have understood what the experience lacked until I had something to contrast it with.

I entered *Writing From Captivity* with a lot of pride over my degree, believing this granted me some special status or gratification. That concert evaporated the first time I struggled to respond to a question posed by Isaac and was reinforced when others in the group proved themselves capable writers and learners. It became increasingly obvious that I needed *Writing From Captivity*, maybe not for critical analyses of carceral literature as much as relearning how to function within a group. Independence has its limits.

Sixteen years of incarceration had blinded me to the way prison stunts social and emotional connections. The walls had cut me off from the outside world in a physical sense but had equally damaging mental manifestations. Beyond daily interactions on the cell block, communicating could be disconcerting. It had been easy to drift away from civilized discourse in our isolated world. An image of

William Golding's *Lord of the Flies* came to mind. What must the adults have thought upon discovering the boys lost on their savage island, with painted faces and readied spears as they hunted Ralph? How, in that moment, as civilization burst the real and imagined wildness eroding the boys' thoughts, some questioned ever losing touch. Others ran off into the jungle, no longer interested in the trappings of society, fully consumed by their brutish existence.

Dr. K brought in a number of guest lecturers from Duke University Divinity School. They spoke on everything from apocryphal writing by Iranian dissidents to the book of Daniel. A lecture on Italian revolutionary Toni Negri, discourse on Nelson Mandela—some of it was interesting from a historical, international perspective of confinement, but I grew frustrated. None of these academics talked about mass incarceration in America or the prison industrial complex. Some guys asked about it and received only, "We're not focusing on that right now." The reason would become clear later.

Writing From Captivity lasted 12 weeks. At the end, Dr. K and Isaac arranged a celebratory meal with a buffet of fried chicken, mashed potatoes with gravy, biscuits, apple pie, and iced tea. Four long, white tables arranged in a large U accommodated the group, which included three new psychologists, Dr. K's immediate boss, Dr. H, the AWOP, and some programs staff who swooped in, loaded up plates and left before any prisoners received food.

The presence of two senior prison officials (Dr. H and the AWOP) and several psychologists gave the meal an uncomfortable vibe. While many of my peers were unconcerned, eating and pocketing food as if they were in the chow hall and unlikely to eat again anytime soon, a few like me watched and listened. Though it was meant to be fun and carefree, this kind of mixed company social gathering had never happened before. Staff didn't eat with prisoners. Fraternization was discouraged on both sides. The new AWOP, Mr. Atkins, looked uncomfortable. My nervousness wasn't overwhelming, but it dampened any appetite I might have had for the array of food. The unusualness of the event, combined with people who, for all of my adult life, symbolized "The Adversary," created a unique situation in which I was forced to examine my prejudices and stereotypes. Maybe the staff did too, and for once saw us as more than our imposed status as "inmates."

Dr. K gave out certificates of completion, shaking hands and congratulating each of us to a round of applause. It all felt odd, embarrassing to be singled out in the very way I wished had happened when I received my diploma. It made me grateful no one applauded then. Smiling faces, general good humor, easy adult conversations about the future—then the warden and deputy warden entered the room.

Dr. K stood and spoke. We had been part of an experiment. Previous wardens forbid the idea of programs on death row. When the new warden, Mr. Lassiter, took over in 2011, he held a different view of prison programs, believing that rehabilitation is important to a safe prison environment.

Providing meaningful activities that promote personal growth, competence, and good self-esteem made it better for everyone. The success of *Writing From Captivity* meant volunteer-led therapeutic programs could be replicated in other prisons.

"Besides that," said Lassiter, "on a more basic level, if I give you things you like it means you behave. When you don't, I take them away. It works better than solitary confinement." He thanked Dr. K and promised more programs would be coming From the Mental Health Department. Everyone applauded. It never crossed my mind how this declaration would be interpreted by Mr. Atkins.

The following spring Dr. K offered several new groups: *Creative Writing, Chess Therapy, Art Therapy, Mindfulness and Meditation,* and *Journaling.* An outside volunteer led each group, boosting interest because they had wholly different attitudes and beliefs toward prisoners. While staff tolerated being around us because it was their job, the volunteers wanted to teach us and learn about life on death row. The volunteers were invested in our rehabilitation regardless of the sentence, but they also knew not everyone believed in that ideal.

I signed up for all the new groups but preferred *Created Writing* and *Journaling.* Writing had become a way to communicate my incarceration experiences to the free world. Before, discussion of the US prison system was avoided so it didn't look like Dr. K was stirring us up. It had been important for the pilot program to succeed without anyone questioning what we learned. Once Dr. K received permission to implement more groups, he relaxed the restrictions on discussion topics (within reason in the natural progression of a given group) and we talked about the criminal justice system at length.

Creative Writing began with Viktor Frankl's *Man's Search for Meaning.* Maturity and education sharpened my understanding of the book and its applications in my life since the first time I read it. In my first decade of incarceration, I stopped looking out of my cell window because seeing a blue sky pierced by swaying green oaks reminded me of a world I could no longer touch. The loss of freedom made it difficult to breathe, a sensation reinforced by razor wire. In the second decade, I narrowed my focus. In the dust of the past lay my understanding of the present. It might be painful, but Frankl reminded me that suffering should be embraced, measured, and mined. In it lay hidden opportunities. I had discovered some, but only a small token in an endless field.

Man's Search for Meaning is "survival literature," but this fails to convey how deeply it changed my incarcerated life. Prison is suffering. Like any form of adversity, it exposes people, leaving no room for "false illusions and artificial optimism," facades of toughness or veneers of virtue. In that naked light, with every flaw revealed, a choice remains, one of existence and identity. Higher education distinguished past and present, awakened my potential, and taught me important skills, but it also made me responsible for the composition of my life in the way any tool in a workman's hands demands use.

The summer of 2014, I enrolled in three advanced paralegal courses from the Center for Legal Studies, through Adams State University: *Intellectual Property* because I wanted to learn more about copyright law *Criminal Procedure*, and *Constitutional Law* to better understand the appellate process. Becoming a paralegal might have been out of reach, but at least I would know enough about the law to keep up with its impact on my life.

Juggling advanced paralegal courses, writing a blog (BeyondSteelDoors.com) with the help of friends on the outside, and attending Dr. K's groups tested my ability to organize tasks. The writing stayed manageable because it was a part of everyday life. I wrote letters, notes and essays for coursework, essays and short stories for Dr. K's Groups, blog posts reflecting on my incarcerated life, and an occasional short story sent to publishers. If it grew difficult, I reminded myself that full-time college students do more with less time and countless distractions.

Dr. K's groups changed the atmosphere on death row. Fewer people went to lock-up. Most of the staff were glad we had constructive activities because it made their job easier. Block tensions dissipated because fewer people were around. Those attending the groups of ten shared what they learned with others who chose not to sign up. Word spread throughout the prison that death row had become an upbeat unit, with staff frequently requesting to be transferred there because it was the safest part of the Central Prison.

In September 2014, the North Carolina Innocence Inquiry Commission exonerated Henry McCollum, who had been on death row for 30 years. Newly uncovered DNA evidence indicated another man, Roscoe Artis, was likely responsible for the 1984 rape and murder of Sabrina Buie. When the crime occurred, 19-year-old Henry and his 15-year-old brother Leon were misidentified as suspects because they were Black and lived in the neighborhood. Detectives from Red Springs Police Department coerced Henry and Leon into confessing. Both brothers were sentenced to death, but in the mid-90s Leon's murder conviction was overturned and he received a life sentence. For nearly 20 years thereafter, Henry's appellate attorneys tried to persuade him to plead guilty and accept LWOP under relief for the intellectually disabled. Henry refused, maintaining his innocence. The Commission does not review capital cases and turned down Henry's original claim. They held that death row prisoners have adequate legal representation throughout the appellate process, though this completely ignores their lack of investigatory and subpoena power, which the Commission has and sets them apart. Henry's attorneys knew of the DNA evidence but had no way to force the police to turn it over for testing. Fortunately, a friend of Leon's filed a claim with the Commission on his behalf. When it decided to investigate the case, it had to investigate Henry's involvement too, ultimately finding both men innocent.

Henry's exoneration shook many on death row because it seemed to come from nowhere. Henry always claimed innocence, but such claims are common in prison and just as commonly disbelieved. Henry's case also appeared to have been open and shut because of his confession, and the horrific nature of the crime. They were the only elements people focused on–law enforcement, prosecutors, jurors, and even U.S. Supreme Court Justice Antonin Scalia who, in response to turning down one of Henry's appeals, used his case as justification for the death penalty. This singular focus ignored key pieces of evidence and facts until the Commission unearthed them. The struggle to understand how Henry wound up on death row is rooted in the popular myths that the State always plays by the rules, is interested in the truth, and if someone goes to prison, they must be guilty.

We grew hopeful after Henry's exoneration. Surely the public would recognize the fallibility of the appellate process and unacceptable risk of executing innocent people and abolish the death penalty. Henry made the eighth innocent person freed from North Carolina's death row–something had to give. Dr. K listened as we talked, expressing insights where he could and empathy when he could not. He talked about helping Henry adjust an automatic seatbelt before leaving Central Prison, a simple technology that didn't exist the last time he sat in a car. Dr. K's willingness to relate the story is one of the many things that set him apart.

One of the benefits of free, volunteer-led programs is how outsiders clamored to instruct us, to participate in the cultural revolution on death row that revealed our humanity. Dr. K told us about it in Creative Writing one day.

"You wouldn't believe how many people want to work with you guys. Whenever I tell someone about our classes they always say 'when can I volunteer? I want to be a part of what y'all have going on.'"

Aside from volunteer instructors, Dr. K frequently brought in guest speakers like he did in *Writing From Captivity*. Each was interesting in his or her own way, but none as famous or impactful as Bryan Stevenson, New York University Law Professor and executive director of the Equal Justice Initiative in Montgomery, Alabama.

I had previously read Bryan Stevenson's book *Just Mercy* and knew enough from that to understand his presence on death row was under the radar. The AWOP, Mr. Atkins, may have known Dr. K brought in guest speakers for our edification, and each guest went through the same security clearance to enter Central Prison, but it was unlikely Atkins really knew who Bryan Stevenson is. If he had, I doubt the influential attorney would have made it into the prison.

As it was, Bryan Stevenson stood in front of a packed multipurpose room (roughly 60 people squeezed into a 20'x20' room), with more people standing in the hallway, and spoke for nearly an hour about two things: proximity and challenging the narrative.

Distance makes capital punishment and mass incarceration possible. People convicted of crimes are depersonalized with labels like "felon" and "criminal," then dehumanized in prison. As State property, prisoners are exiled from society. Their alleged crimes justification for the worst treatment imaginable, the pain they suffer defined as "justice" for the victim. For the incarcerated innocents who gain freedom there is no apology, merely the false claim their wrongful imprisonment is an acceptable risk or indication the system works. This is the American "justice" system, the narrative disseminated by journalists to embed the public consciousness. This narrative denies any responsibility for the injustices committed against the poor, minority, and marginalized. Challenging it means making the public aware there are human beings in prison, not animals.

Dr. K challenged the narrative by pushing prison officials to change the way people are treated in solitary confinement, on death row and the mental health unit. Viktor Frankl taught millions of people about the Jews' experiences in Nazi concentration camps, making them understand that suffering is universal but can be the foundation of a meaningful existence.

"Show people what you are, not who you were" Bryan Stevenson told us. "Prove you are more than a moment in time. More than your worst mistakes. More than a body in a prison cell. Challenge the narrative told about your life in any way you can."

The path forward grew more distinct. *Writing From Captivity* would be a natural way to challenge the narrative and help people understand what it really means to be confined.

11

CULTURAL SHIFT

Dr. K's programs improved life on death row, creating a positive learning environment with constructive outlets for stress and anxiety. Programs occupied prisoners who might otherwise have caused problems for staff or declined into mental illness. The lack of trouble made life in prison safer for everyone. Yet, some prisoners resented the programs because they feared opening themselves to good things, then having their joy stolen. Bitterness became a defense mechanism. Some staff resented the programs because they believe their job is to make us suffer. Vengeance, not rehabilitation, is their primary philosophy whatever the cause, this baked-in hardness created a pocket of opposition to Dr. K's groups.

Not every prison officer or official fed into the undercurrent of animosity. It took individual experiences between them and those of us participating in the groups before attitudes softened. For those it did not, antipathy was carried out in the day-to-day application of policy and minor acts of obstruction.

Staff who read this might claim it's all lies and exaggeration, that they treat us better than we "deserve" or need a heavy hand to keep prisoners in line. It could be worse, they might argue. This is true. It has been worse. Sometimes abusive staff cycle in and out of prison like recidivists, trading facilities when they get caught, or in some circumstances gaining rank.

In 2013, Dr. K received permission to implement changes on Unit One, Central Prison's notorious solitary confinement wing. It came in the wake of a successful class-action lawsuit that claimed staff were physically and psychologically abusing prisoners in the hole. Prisoners handcuffed behind the back were pushed down flights of stairs, beaten with boots, stomped on, chained to a bunk and denied water, starved, and degraded on a regular basis. The excuse staff used? They deserve it. To be clear: regardless of one's crimes, people in State custody

DOI: 10.4324/9781003449454-15

have a constitutional right to humane treatment. They are entitled to it. A federal judge agreed, ordering new safety and security protocols that included cameras on every cellblock, the removal of staff named in the suit, and direct oversight by the court ("Lawsuit: Eight inmates Beaten at NC Prison" By Micheal Biesicker, WRAL.com: May 10, 2013; "NC Prison Warden Promoted After Alleged Beatings," Greensboro News, AP. May 31, 2013).

Dr. K spearheaded many of those reforms, which included de-escalation training for staff whose go-to response was use-of-force, new mental health and suicide prevention procedures, reduced use of solitary confinement, and a Therapeutic Division Unit to transition prisoners from long-term solitary confinement back to the general population. Dr. K represented an end to unchecked abuses on Unit One, but he also signaled a cultural shift toward our right to humane treatment. Yet, there would always be opposition to such efforts.

My studies in literature, philosophy, psychology, criminology, and law helped me better understand and describe this dynamic. Being convicted of and sentenced for a crime involves a complex, flawed, and arbitrary legal process, but it does not preclude certain rights. Conditions of confinement, for example, often ignore the Eighth Amendment's prohibition against cruel and unusual punishment. That is largely because cruelty is customary. Comprehending and intelligently resisting this means drawing a connection between historical justification for mass incarceration and current penal philosophy well enough to challenge it. Complaining about prison and abuse is useless if I cannot articulate and support a position with evidence. My higher education is one type of evidence. Dr. K's programs are another.

Some of Dr. K's groups taught remedial social etiquette, self-expression, social awareness, teamwork, creativity, and communication. Groups were open to everyone. *Hidden Voices* was the one exception. Dr. K pulled me aside one day and asked if I would be interested in an intense writing group where the essays would contribute to a larger project. Because the writing would touch on deeply personal childhood and adolescent experiences, only six competent writers would be selected for the group. Lynden, the lead volunteer and director of *Hidden Voices*, provided positive feedback to essays we wrote from prompts like: favorite childhood memory, childhood mentor, first interaction with law enforcement, and painful childhood memory. Lynden explained that his organization facilitated the creative expression of marginalized groups. Our stories would illustrate the school-to-prison pipeline, systematic racism, and humanity on death row as a way to become involved in the conversation about criminal justice reform. On a more personal level, our writing helped us tap into the past to help understand the present.

By spring of 2015, our work with *Hidden Voices* developed into an art project exhibited at the "Re-Visioning Justice in America Conference," hosted by Vanderbilt Divinity School. Over two dozen speakers and nearly as many events covered everything from the religious roots of incarceration and restorative justice to the death penalty and prison abolition. For the six of us contributing through *Hidden Voices*, the conference seemed vaguely exciting, but disconnected from our reality.

Titled "Serving Life: Transforming Death Row," the *Hidden Voices* exhibit displayed handcrafted life-map displays of our individual paths to prison. My map was a 3-D model of institutions that influenced my life: family, church, school, youth detention, rehab, mental health, and prison. The projects were eventually shared at other colleges and universities, including Guilford College and Duke University.

While *Hidden Voices* met every other week, Ms. Demetral's drama group met every Wednesday. A bubbly, good-natured social worker who minored in theatre, Ms. D had us read *Hamlet, Othello, Antigone*, and *The Crucible*. We discussed key themes in each, watched a video of the play, then wrote an essay describing what we learned. Having aced *Critical Approaches to Drama* for my associate degree, I enjoyed the plays. Much like humanities courses that require reading and analyzing classic literature, Ms. D required attention to perspectives other than your own, reminding that the world has many cultures, but we all share human experiences.

One day Ms. D came in with a new stack of scripts.

"Listen up, people! We're reading Reginald Rose's *12 Angry Men*, then we're gonna watch a DVD. Then, instead of a paper, each of you will pick a character and try out for it, because ... we are going to put on our own production of *12 Angry Men*!"

Crickets. Nervous laughter. A few snorts.

A 1950s drama set in an unnamed metropolis, *12 Angry Men* was a case of an all-white jury deciding the fate of a minority youth accused of killing his father. There were obvious parallels between the prejudice and legal misinformation that plagued capital juries in the 1950s, and capital juries in modern North Carolina. Many of the Black prisoners in our drama group were convicted and sentenced by an all-white jury.

In the play, delinquent minorities were labeled "menaces to society" and the cause of violent crime in the city. One juror remarked "slums are breeding grounds for criminals" as if economic inequality and poverty can be blamed on those who suffer from it and lash out in frustration. *12 Angry Men* may have been written over half a century before, but it expressed the same mentality of the tough-on-crime era and Clintons "superpredators." Fiction reflected the reality of bigotry, ignorance, and systematic racism in courtrooms. Henry McCollum and Leon Brown were Black youth living in a poverty-stricken area of North Carolina. They too experienced the rush to judgment illustrated in *12 Angry Men*. Unfortunately, there was no conscientious juror present in 1985 to spare them from a wrongful conviction and death sentence.

When the time came, Ms. D cast me as the understudy for Juror #3, the primary antagonist in *12 Angry Men*, I didn't expect to be in the play and was genuinely glad to be an understudy. It gave me more time to focus on *Constitutional Law, Intellectual Property*, and *Criminal Procedure*. The advanced paralegal courses, essays for *Hidden Voices*, and blog posts for BeyondSteel-Doors.com was a lot of writing.

Five weeks into rehearsals, and a month out from the first performance, the prisoner playing Juror #3 went to lock-up (accused of a sexual relationship with a female officer). Suddenly the role became my responsibility.

"Can you be ready?" asked Ms. D, concerned because Dr. K had been advertising the production. Word spread fast and plenty of staff were eager to see it. When I nodded, Ms. D narrowed her eyes. "Good," she smiled, trusting me to get it done.

I have never been good at memorizing anything. Exams were more difficult as a result. Except this was different. Everyone depended on my ability to catch up, in part, said one friend: "Because you're educated and know what's at stake." I did. The consequences of failure would be immediate and brutally public, but more than that, like Dr. K's first group, *Writing From Captivity*, this was an opportunity to prove we were all capable of a positive, collaborative project for the betterment of everyone on death row.

Comprehending psychological theory or a U.S. Supreme Court ruling is wholly different from verbatim recitation of dialogue or acting. My approach was simple: if I could earn a degree then memorizing a play should be easy. A Muslim friend showed me some techniques, one of the other jurors quizzed me on lines and cues, but in the end, it came down to repetition. Word-by-word, cue-by-cue, line-by-line. I repeated the parts until they came naturally, and I didn't need the script. I shouted and raged on cue, scowled in the mirror, and drew from a deep well of real anger that everyone who is locked away from their family and loved ones has. When the time arrived for our first performance, I was ready.

The stage was a taped-off corner of an empty cell block on death row. Twelve jurors sat behind two long tables set at a wide angle; on the wall behind us, a large three-part city-scape drawn in chalk by members of the art group. Magazines with emergency scripts taped on them littered the tables, but no one needed them. Ms. D wanted us to wear suits, but the warden nixed the idea, only to relent on ties worn over our crimson jumpsuits. The prop knife was a novelty switch-blade comb, with the comb wrapped in tin-foil, over fifty chairs were available for the audience.

No one could have predicted the response to the death row production of *12 Angry Men*.

In the first performance the front rows were filled with mental health and programs staff, the deputy warden, and associate warden of programs. The remaining seats filled with death row prisoners. Audience a blur, I focused on my lines and cues. For the duration of the play (about 47 minutes on average), I was an angry bigot on a jury in a capital case involving an innocent youth. Imagining myself as the antagonist came naturally because as an RPG Game Master (also called a D&D Dungeon Master), I played all of the antagonists in a campaign. Absorption in the story was part of the fun. It wasn't lost on me that most of us played an RPG. Maybe that's why we did so well.

Loud applause and a few whistles surprised us into smiles. Teary-eyed gratitude from Ms. D followed a speech from the unit manager, Mr. Norris, who expressed pride and excitement for the future:

"You guys represented yourselves and Unit-3 well. Better than anyone could have expected. Keep it up. I promise more will come."

By the third showing, the warden, NCDPS secretary of communications, director of mental health services for North Carolina prisons, secretary for the director of prisons ("The director sends his apologies, but supports all you are doing"), director of rehabilitative services for North Carolina prisons, and several other unnamed prison officials watched our performance of *12 Angry Men*.

Maybe the most significant part of the whole experience is that afterward each prison official shook our hands, congratulated us, and engaged in a few minutes of small talk in which they reiterated support for programs like this throughout North Carolina prisons. Our interaction with those officials was unheard of, and we did our best to press commitments to more programs like GED class, but in the end, they were bureaucrats beholden to the NCDPS secretary, Erik Hooks, and whichever way politics of the moment shifted. For the moment it was in our favor.

By the fifth performance, two superintendents from other NC prisons and a representative from the Department of Juvenile Justice came to watch *12 Angry Men*. Afterward, we discussed the need for and success of Dr. K's programs. One superintendent from a medical custody prison struggling to control the spread of gangs, said:

"You guys were awesome. Your teamwork is outstanding. It's exactly what we need at Maury Correctional. If any y'all get off the row, contact Maury. I've got a place for leaders like y'all."

The other superintendent echoed the need for mature role models among the "young, stubborn hotheads" at Bertie Correctional: "Programs are essential. But programs that don't cost money and are effective? That's a game changer."

At our final 2015 performance of *12 Angry Men*, representatives from the national non-profit Vera Institute of Justice described the moment as "historic" for death row and "indicative of the transformative nature of rehabilitative programs in prison." We were pleased and overwhelmed by the positive responses. They gave us real hope the penal system would change.

Though *12 Angry Men* went on a break, plenty of other programs continued. Our *Hidden Voices* vignettes evolved into the stage play *Serving Life*. Lynden told us our writing would take on a new focus as we went along, but performing a play of our own making felt surreal. Writing stories about child and adolescent turmoil, abuse, and incarceration is different from acting it out in front of strangers. We each faced embarrassing moments.

Poverty, addiction, family dysfunction, mental illness, and the blocked economic opportunity that often leads to criminality were on full display in *Serving Life*. Our humanity was the focus, but like *12 Angry Men*, no explicit statement condemned the death penalty, racial injustice or the criminal legal system's dysfunction. I found fault with this but understood the need for subtlety in a play performed on death row.

Rehearsing and performing *Serving Life* was different from *12 Angry Men*. My lines were shorter and less frequent, the greater focus on race pushing me, the only white prisoner, to the side. There was also a great deal of conflict between some of the actors, due in part to old hatreds and ego. The drama within the drama made practices burdensome. After the first few performances, two of the actors vowed never to do another.

The content of *Serving Life* made many in the audience cry. Some prison officials grew uncomfortable, others didn't show up at all. The raw emotion of our stories made prison staff see us more as human beings, but it also seemed to draw smaller audiences than *12 Angry Men*. Either way, it was nonetheless a success.

The plays did a lot to change how prison staff perceived death row. It seemed as if we finally made a positive impact on our "community," enough that on doctor's appointments outside the Unit, medical and programs staff made it a habit to greet some of us in the hallway. Staff on the Unit were more relaxed and communicative. It may have still been prison, but compared to previous years and administrations past, the time was more manageable.

I finished the advanced paralegal courses in the spring of 2016 and planned to register for three more to complete the Advanced Paralegal Certificate. Two things stopped me. First, I discovered that, while paralegal courses provided transferable credit hours, the certificate held no significance. Second, I received an Ohio University newsletter advertising a scholarship opportunity for incarcerated students. The potential of winning a scholarship meant more than simply a monetary award; it would be external validation of my academic ability.

Offered by the Alpha Sigma Lambda Honor Society, the scholarship provided for three Ohio University courses. Specific to adult learners, it recognized scholastic achievement and leadership in the student's career field. It was a prize unlike any I had ever considered attaining or thought myself capable of striving toward.

Students were required to be enrolled in an Ohio University course, have completed a minimum of 36 OU credits, have a minimum 3.2 GPA and financial need for assistance. Applications also had to include a personal statement and faculty letters of recommendation. Each ASL chapter would select its two best applicants to compete for 14 available scholarships. The Alpha Sigma Lambda Honor Society maintained chapters in 50 colleges and universities.

Winning the ASL scholarship did not seem like a stretch for my imagination because my self-concept is no longer tied to failure. The mentally ill drug addict who entered the criminal legal system in 1997 as an ignorant teenager no longer existed. As an educated, spiritual adult my life held purpose. Could I win a scholarship? My transformative journey thus far seemed to indicate one answer.

Yes.

12

LEARNING ENVIRONMENT

In June 2016, the prison administration had a phone installed on every death row cell block. It looked like a pay phone without coin slots: a rectangular steel box bolted to the wall with a steel-encased cable and bulky black receiver. You could purchase minutes from the canteen, call collect, have someone on the outside put money on your phone account, or call someone who established an account with the GTL network. Each call cost $1.89 for 15 minutes, a cheaper amount than most jails, which often charge $15.00 for 15 minutes.

Up until this point, North Carolina death row prisoners received one 10-minute collect call around Christmas. Installation of the phone came after an extensive campaign by family and friends, who advocated on our behalf to the director of prisons and other officials. The director of prisons relented, in part, because of the positive things coming from death row and our ability to rise to the moment.

Using the phone again was challenging at first. It had been over 17 years since I used a phone with any regularity. In the meantime, my only method of communication occurred via letters. Sometimes this worked, but unless you are an effective writer, letters lose a lot of emotion, nuance, and urgency. Over time, unless you are a dedicated writer, and the average person is not, maintaining a close relationship is unlikely, and if you need a quick response to a question? Forget about it.

My conversations on the phone were halting and awkward, out of sync with the brief delay in the line. After a while, it got better, as did my relationship with my aging parents, who struggled to write or visit. Connecting with pen pals was also challenging because it meant navigating a conversation beyond the lines and margins of a few pages. It meant that constantly evolving relationships and instantaneous communication that had been missing from my life for a long time.

DOI: 10.4324/9781003449454-16

After strengthening relationships with family and friends, the phone advanced my higher education. I wrote to Haning Hall, home of Ohio University's academic advising office, for a new course catalog and registration forms. They customarily assign an advisor with enrollment in new courses, but this time the office number was relevant. Past academic advisors were reluctant communicators by mail, which made troubleshooting simple problems an arduous process.

I called my advisor's number to introduce myself. Kyle answered on the second ring, polite, welcoming, and interested in talking about my education. Expert direction and advice on which courses to pursue, what would be needed for the ASL scholarship application, how to register for the Bachelor of Specialized Studies degree program ... within the space of a few phone calls, Kyle provided more useful information than all of my other previous academic advisors combined. Talking with Kyle filled a number of gaps in my education I didn't know existed until she spoke. Most importantly, she provided direct support and mentorship that unlocked my potential in ways I never imagined.

One of the first things Kyle did was assess my abilities by administering the Cliffton Strengths Inventory, a personality measure that reveals an individual's top five strengths. Ordinarily given by employers and career coaches, the Cliffton Strengths Inventory helps people tap core strengths for better productivity and greater levels of success. More recently used by academic advisors, it can help students understand the motivation and structure of their potential. On the phone I answered over one hundred multiple-choice questions about how I interpreted or might respond to a given scenario. My choices, like most personality measures, displayed patterns of thought represented by a key "theme" or strength.

Completion of the Cliffton Strengths Inventory generated a "Strengths Insight Report" and "Action Planning Guide." Where the report defined and explained what my strengths meant, the guide outlined the best ways to foster and use them as tools to achieve goals. My five key theme descriptions listed in order of prominence:

1. Strategic: "People who are especially talented in the Strategic theme create alternative ways to proceed. Faced with any given scenario, they can quickly spot the relevant patterns and issues."
2. Analytical: "People who are especially talented in the Analytical theme search for reasons and causes. They have the ability to think about all the factors that might affect a situation."
3. Input: "People who are especially talented in the Input theme have a craving to know more. Often they like to collect and archive all kinds of information."
4. Learner: "People who are especially talented in the Learner theme have a great desire to learn and want to continuously improve. In particular, the process of learning, rather than the outcome, excites them."
5. Restorative: "People who are especially talented in the Restorative theme are adept at dealing with problems. They are good at figuring out what is wrong and resolving it."

The accompanying in-depth analysis of each theme gave new meaning to the phrase "know thyself."

The year 2017 brought a change in prison administrators. For the past two years, Warden Joyner supported Dr. K's groups and facilitated the cultural shift at Central Prison. A local journalist quoted the new warden, Mr. Thomas, as saying the most important thing in corrections is "Security, Security, Security." Where Mr. Joyner had a background in programs, Mr. Thomas was the former head of Internal Affairs (IA) and a Disciplinary Hearing Officer (the DHO is responsible for adjusting rules violations that determine the length of stays in solitary confinement). Mr. Joyner maintained an administration that adhered to his philosophy; so did Mr. Thomas.

This included unit management. Mr. Norris was replaced by Mr. Jeuhrs, a career prison guard who said his job was to ensure people on death row are executed (despite the fact there has been a moratorium on executions in North Carolina since 2006). Both Jeuhrs and Thomas attended our final performance of *Serving Life*. Afterward, as we had before, we shook hands with the attending prison staff. Forgetting that not everyone was committed to the cultural shift on death row, I shook Mr. Joyner's hand, then Mr. Thomas's hand, thanking them for coming. When I got to Jeuhrs he stood there, hands in pockets, and looked me up and down. That look said it all: things were about to change.

Kyle helped me apply for the ASL scholarship by typing up my personal statement and submitting the paperwork to the ASL chapter counselor, but I faced a few hurdles.

First, my application required a letter of recommendation from university faculty. Correspondence courses do not create much opportunity to establish a rapport with instructors. Sometimes I finished courses where the only words written by the professor was a "Good Job!" on my final course report. However, the letter of recommendation did not specify which university, so I asked Lynden. She taught me at Duke University and had worked with me closely over the last year. She readily agreed.

The next problem was my lack of any noticeable leadership role. I tried to start a GED program on death row, collecting the names of 22 persons who needed and wanted to earn a GED, researching an estimated cost of texts and tests per person, and writing several prison officials about the idea. What I discovered was discouraging. Ms. Stackey, a programs case manager, used to run the GED program at Central Prison. She told me that when testing went completely online in 2014, prison officials decided prisoners would have to get their GED at a lower-security prison facility. Wake Tech, a local community college that previously taught the GED class at Central Prison in years past, still did so at other facilities. Ms. Stackey suggested I write and ask the warden.

Ms. Thomas's reply put an end to my GED campaign:

> The GED program at Central Prison has been discontinued. Inmates desiring to earn a GED must reach the appropriate security level to do so. Death row inmates are not at Central Prison to be educated.

It did not matter that I asked to establish a privately funded GED program and was ready to do all the organizing. Nor did it seem to matter that all these people had appeals likely to get their sentence reduced someday. The warden's letter also made me fear for the future of my own education, but I could not let it slow me down.

The third problem with my ASL scholarship was a low GPA. I never thought a day would arrive when my grade point average mattered in prison, but now it did. For any scholarship, a 3.3 GPA is not competitive. Part of the problem was an F I received in a business law course for credit by examination. I disputed the grade and tried to appeal it, but one of my previous advisors neglected to follow through on the appeal. Once the grade became part of my OU transcript, it dropped my GPA.

Regardless of these disadvantages, I wrote a strong personal essay describing the activities and achievements I believed qualified me as a potential scholarship recipient.

It only took a month to discover my scholarship application failed to make it past the chapter selection round.

Prisons are like fiefdoms, where wardens act like feudal lords, prison staff their court and guard, and prisoners the lowly serfs. From one facility to the next, management styles and rehabilitative programs, or lack thereof, vary. Some facilities are more violent because there are insufficient programs and guards with a punitive, abusive approach toward incarcerated persons. Other facilities are calm, have mental health and limited educational programs, and staff are an invisible reminder instead of a frequently used club. Because Central Prison became a prison where people are processed to and from other facilities, we often heard about these differences. "Camps," as correctional institutions are referred to, with less violence and more programs are "sweet spots," a place everyone wants to serve their sentence. Sweet spots often have a waiting list for transfers. Other facilities with gang violence, high suicide rates, and brutal guards are referred to by name alone. "Don't go to Alexander, Micheal Anthony Kerr died of dehydration in solitary."

Maybe, at one time, North Carolina prisons were governed like identical parts of a system, which kept the dysfunction from spreading, but everything changed in the 90s when parole and access to higher education ended. By setting a draconian tone with longer sentences and warehousing, pockets of resistance to this new correctional philosophy dwindled. Sweet spots became rare. A consistent lack of effective, professional management pervaded the penal system.

Independent oversight could have addressed unsafe conditions of confinement, abuse, undertraining, and understaffing before they become overwhelming signs of neglect. But there was none. Such was the state of North Carolina prisons when Bertie Correctional Officer Megan Callahan was killed in 2017.

The change in attitude amongst staff was immediate. Though the murder of Officer Callahan occurred in a medium custody facility with open dorms and more freedom of movement, it affected every North Carolina prison. Central Prison, the state's only maximum-security facility and home to death row, required its staff to travel in pairs and volunteers had to sit by the exit of any room in which a prisoner stood. Greater vigilance brought more searches. For some staff the new security protocols seemed like unnecessary work. They quietly complained after a while that the overreaction by prison officials added to the problem. Officers who dared voice such opinions were reprimanded. Some staff quit. The Warden, Internal Affairs (IA), and unit management tightened control by enforcing every policy to the letter, launching frivolous investigations, and fostering an almost neurotic suspicion of anyone resisting this punitive turn.

The end of Dr. K's programs began with one of the new security protocols. During a group an officer usually sat in a chair outside of the multipurpose room and watched through plexiglass windows. Sometimes, they sat in on sessions if invited and even participated in the discussion. That stopped. Staff had to be in the room with any volunteer. While this grated at times, it served to remind us that prison is about control and we had none.

It happened on a day we were about to meet for *Hidden Voices*. Five of us in the group, which expanded to 12 from the original six, were called to the sergeant's office. When my name was announced over the intercom, I thought nothing of it and reported to the office. Walking in, an IA officer handcuffed me and two other members of *Hidden Voices* as the Unit Manager and Lt. Soucler, head of Internal Affairs, watched. Within minutes they put us in solitary, under "investigation."

Putting prisoners under investigation does not mean they have been charged with violating policy, merely that suspicion surrounds their behavior, and they are guilty until proven innocent. The duration of the investigation depends on the alleged offense, the credibility of any attached information, who initiated the investigation, and whether it's legitimate or an attempt by prison officials to send a message. Some prisoners who manage to elude the DHO with wrongdoing or anger at the warden have been put in solitary, under investigation, without charges, for nearly a year before getting released or charged. Investigations often result in long-term solitary (six months or more) but are more commonly used as a catch-all, a one-size fits any kind of transgression punishment.

One of the hardest parts about the hole, other than utter hopelessness, is the lack of information. Hours feel like days. No one from IA came to interview me or the others. Days passed. I feared the potential impact on my education as horror stories about months-long investigations came to mind. I thought about all my activities for the previous six months, hoping to glean a clue.

I had some small success getting essays published in the *J Journal* (a quarterly publication from the John Jay College of Criminal Justice), *The Marshall Project*, and *Scalawag Magazine* (a southern social justice and civil rights publication). My writing did not attack prison officials or otherwise incite or provoke or antagonize; rather, as Lynden and others taught, I expressed experience. With regular access to the phone this even extended into podcast interviews on *Red Letter Christians* and *Talking Bull*. My main concern revolved around a collaborative project called *Life Lines Collective*.

Life Lines was a recording app created by two ministers on the outside, one of whom formerly volunteered for Dr. K's *Creative Writing* group. Five or six of us dialed a phone number to access an automated app that recorded up to ten minutes of audio. Spoken word, poetry, and essays were then edited and published on the LifeLines.is website. Even though we had no direct internet access I thought IA might find this a suspicious use of the phone. Considering prison phones record every conversation for review by prison officials, this seemed plausible.

Not knowing made my time on Unit One painful and anxious. Due process and internal disciplinary procedures have only a loose relationship. Without access to the phone, I quickly grew to rely on, and my outgoing mail being screened, I had no way to effectively communicate what occurred with friends and family. I was also nearing a final exam for *Accounting*—what if I missed the deadline? What would my sponsor think? Had I built up enough integrity and trust to convince the people who supported me that this was not my doing? Responsibility had become central to my higher education; it did not allow for finger-pointing. Irrational fear turned my stomach. No more collaborative projects. They were too easily misconstrued as conspiring or whatever else IA thought we did. Nothing could be allowed to jeopardize continuing my higher education. Nothing.

After a little more than a week it ended as suddenly as it began. We returned to Unit 3 without charges or explanation. I wanted to know what happened. Needed to understand why. I asked to speak with the unit manager, and he told me.

An officer sitting in a *Hidden Voices* session overheard one of the volunteers say to several of us, "I love y'all." The officer had been told to report any suspicious activity to Jeuhrs. The volunteer's "love" was "undue familiarity," an accusation usually linked to prison staff who fraternized with prisoners, but seemingly included volunteers. It was all Jeuhrs needed to initiate an investigation of the volunteers, Dr. K, and several of us from *Hidden Voices* who happened to be in the room.

Jeuhrs bluntly said, "We can't have some doctor running around the prison thinking he can do anything he wants. Thinking he doesn't have to answer to anyone. Having inmates thinking it's okay to have volunteers say they 'love' them."

We were released from the hole after Dr. K's volunteers—about a dozen—refused to come in and be questioned by Lt. Soucrer or otherwise participate in the investigation. IA went rabid. A full audit of Dr. K's budget and program revealed no wrongdoing, but this did not prevent the harassment of mental health staff. Within a month the psychologists and interns trained by Dr. K left Central Prison to work elsewhere. Dr. K followed shortly thereafter.

Punitive prison culture, driven by Warden Thomas, Lt. Soucrer, Jeuhrs, and like-minded anti-intellectuals, reasserted itself. Dr. K's programs had generated a real hope prison officials would invest in the rehabilitative ideal again. That hope left with Dr. K and his staff. Without programs, more people went to Unit One and the level of animosity between staff and prisoners increased.

Around this time investigative reporting by the *Charlotte Observer* journalist Ames Alexander (among others) uncovered rampant corruption amongst staff who brought in drugs and cellphones or participated in gang activity. Suicides were at a national high. Assaults on staff had increased, and the decay of North Carolina's penal system could no longer be ignored or quickly fixed.

The breakdown ultimately killed more prison staff. In August 2017 four prisoners at Pasquotank Correctional Institute attempted an escape and killed four prison officers in the process. What had already been a slow boil of legislative outrage after the investigative reporting turned into calls for the national guard, an immediate resumption of executions, and rhetoric about cracking down on prisoners who dared assault staff. When an investigation into the cases of death was conducted, the focus remained on security and staffing.

It should have been predicted decades before that eliminating support for rehabilitative programs and parole would have repercussions. The myth that "nothing works" became an iron fist used to bludgeon and denigrate the incarcerated. Venom replaced concern for the future. Public safety and rehabilitation were buried beneath the national rhetoric of being tough on crime. Prisons became more violent, fewer staff wanted to work there for little more than fast food wages. Lower pay, less training, and people who often lacked a higher education overseeing a human warehouse filled with social ills ... the signs had been there for years, but lawmakers ignored them. What happened at Pasquotank should have left prison officials asking how they could have missed the obvious. However, doing so would mean admitting responsibility for maintaining the carceral state, or at least acknowledging the needs of people in prison.

Most college students attend regular classes on a safe campus. Their learning environment is stable and mundane; their social environment generally fun and stimulating. Prison is none of these things. Dangerous, oppressive, hostile, and regressive, the worst part about prison is that the public believes this is a deserved condition of existence for anyone convicted of a crime. Human rights, or constitutional ones, rarely matter. The fact that it makes fiscal and public safety sense to provide education and skills necessary for reentry does not seem to matter. Absolute punishment blocks these needs. Yet, in this desert a number of good people have contributed to my education. Through them I gained access to some profound knowledge that shaped the person I became in prison. But the most important lesson was taught in the absence of good teachers, the negative space where most people wither. The egregious failures of prison to address crime or make communities safe or cure what ails society awakened me to the purpose of my life.

> When you see something that's not right you have a moral obligation to say something. To do something.
>
> *Rep. John Lewis*

13

CHALLENGING THE NARRATIVE

After I finished the accounting course, Kyle sent an application for Ohio University's Bachelor of Specialized Studies degree program. Up until this point I chose courses based on the Degree Audit Report and what grabbed my attention. Where the DAR was a general guide, the BSS application forced me to map out specific courses that fulfilled my area of concentration in the social sciences and organize any remaining required courses at the junior and senior levels. As a multidisciplinary degree program, the BSS application also required a Goal Statement and Statement of Rationale.

> Who are you as a student?
> What educational goals do you have within the BSS program?
> Where will you go after graduating?

Answering these questions meant setting aside my status as a prisoner, ignoring the uncertainty of my future, and investing in a purpose for my higher education beyond its intrinsic value. The goals I set for myself would determine who I am as a student and what happened after graduation. It expected success. I had been labeled "State Property" for most of my life. As such, it presumed failure. Though I had already embraced academic achievement as a way of life, the BSS degree program application was a formal agreement acknowledging that embrace.

> How will the B.S.S. program help you reach your goals?
> Expand my knowledge. Increase my credibility. Develop my leadership. Demonstrate my ability to overcome.

DOI: 10.4324/9781003449454-17

As my writing about and understanding of the criminal legal system grew more informed, and my work with *Hidden Voices* personalized that writing, publication became more frequent. *Prison Writes*, the *Marshall Project*, and *Scalawag Magazine* published a number of my essays, and though these successes felt good, I knew more needed to be done.

One day while talking with my friend Jennifer, a former volunteer with *Hidden Voices*, she mentioned sharing my writing with her husband, Frank Baumgartner, and that he wanted to talk. Dr. Baumgartner taught political science and the University of North Carolina at Chapel Hill and occasionally led student tours through Central Prison. I agreed to call him.

Dr. Baumgartner explained that he showed my *Scalawag* magazine article *Life without Parole is Silent Execution* with his POLI203 class *Race, Innocence, and the End of the Death Penalty*. The students responded positively, asking questions about the similarities between life imprisonment and death, and sparking discussions that spanned several classes. During our conversation Dr. Baumgartner asked me a question that had the potential to change the course and application of my education, a crossroads much like the one presented by Father Dan:

"Say, Lyle, what do you think about maybe calling into class and speaking with the students about your writing and experiences?"

I immediately recognized it as an opportunity to pull back the curtain on our isolated, often ignored carceral world; a chance to talk about higher education and push back against the false belief that life without parole is any kind of mercy. This was the front line of reform, a gap in understanding into which I had to change.

The students read several of my published articles and the North Carolina Supreme Court's decision on my direct appeal (a review of constitutional errors at my trial). From their reading the students then generated a list of questions, read to me over the phone by Dr. Baumgartner a few weeks before the scheduled call. Talking to students was a great responsibility and I wanted to prove myself worthy. What I said could impact how they thought about capital punishment and how the criminal legal system really works. To avoid missing any important points or come off sounding uncertain, I wrote a speech. Leaning into my writing skills seemed a safe way to facilitate the interaction and make the most of it. Every word mattered. Though it made me nervous, so many people wanted to hear my thoughts on carceral policy, I believed myself capable enough to fulfill the moment.

The day of the call squeezed me with a different kind of anxiety. Despite the structure of most prisons, it is also a place where anything that can go wrong often does. A number of things could cause a lockdown and prevent me from accessing the phone: a fight, a tornado drill, medical emergency, an assault on staff, maintenance coming through the block to fix a commode, door or light; each reason enough to disrupt the scheduled call. Each played out in my mind until tension clenched my jaw.

I called at one o'clock on a Tuesday.

Dr. Baumgartner answered, "Hi there, Lyle. We're ready when you are."

In the background, a few papers rustled. Someone coughed. Is this what nearly three hundred quiet undergraduate students sounded like? Heart thrumming, short of breath, I pushed aside my fear and spoke.

"Thank you for giving me the chance to speak to you today. First, let me answer the most important question you asked: What is the single greatest reform needed in the system?"

I had less than 15 minutes to convey what took years of hard lessons to learn. They needed to understand how higher education transformed me from a reckless, mentally ill delinquent, someone incapable of holding a job or paying rent, into a responsible, goal-oriented adult focused on leaving the world a better place and making positive contributions to society. Maybe the whole story would take too long, but at least, for now, I could open a small window.

"Higher education can no longer be viewed as a privilege. By maintaining this status quo and limiting college to those who are free and can afford it, a permanent underclass will continue to fill America's prisons. Educating prisoners can help end the poverty of thought that begets crime and violence. We represent the most needy and marginalized sub-citizens in the U.S. To break this cycle there must be greater investment in the idea that people go to prison to learn a lesson. They go to learn how to become civilized human beings and productive citizens. What good is confinement for public safety if most of the incarcerated are released back into the community less skilled, more stigmatized, and desperate?"

Confidence replaced anxiety as my words gained momentum. These were not just my experiences but the shared experiences of millions. Their history and voices strengthened mine. During a second 15-minute call Dr. Baumgartner briefly discussed my capital trial, remarking on the inequity of a younger, adolescent defendant being sentenced to death when the older equally culpable co-defendant received a plea deal and release from prison for cooperating with the State. My responses were careful and brief; these calls were about educating the public, not retrying my case.

After my call ended, my mind swirled with the potential of teaching people about the criminal legal system. I had felt useless for so long, yet here was a more satisfying use of my skill as a writer and experience as a form of expertise. Until now, "how" I could be a contributing member of society seemed just beyond reach. While writing is one method, it often felt disconnected, like throwing money down a well and wishing people understood. Directly interacting with students, hearing their curiosity, and feeling their comprehension was everything I hoped for and more. I immediately wanted to do it again.

Kyle and my oldest friend, Tara, helped send my resume and letter of reference from Dr. Baumgartner to professors at other universities. We connected with Dr. Joshua Page, a criminology instructor at the University of Minnesota, Minneapolis, then Dr. Amanda Cox, a criminology instructor at

Ohio University, Athens. Both responded with interest to my query about speaking in their classrooms, scheduling tentative dates to work toward that goal. Over the summer, Dr. Cox agreed to use some of my writing to teach her online senior capstone course *The Death Penalty in the United States*, with a speaking event scheduled for the following spring when she taught the course in person. Dr. Page set up a speaking agreement for late fall. Then my environment reasserted itself.

In June 2018, Lt. Soucrer, unit manager of Central Prison's hospital, former head of Internal Affairs, and an "enforcer" for two previous wardens was beaten and stabbed until he nearly died. Considering the rising level of animosity between some staff and prisoners, and Soucrer's background, the attack surprised no one. Prior to working in North Carolina prisons, Soucrer was fired by Vermont Department of Corrections for pistol-whipping a handcuffed prisoner. Little changed when he worked for Central Prison. As a Unit One sergeant, Soucrer was responsible for some of the most egregious abuses detailed in the 2013 lawsuit. Rather than be fired, though, he gained rank.

Soucrer's background and the administration's response depicts the common tough-on-crime-at-all-costs penal philosophy that accepts violence toward prisoners. It is still the sort of behavior for which Abu Ghraib guards became infamous, partly because many had worked in American prison systems. The attack on Soucrer wasn't just retaliation against an abusive prison officer; it also signaled an inflection point in an increasingly violent population. Prison officials recognized this when, for several weeks after, staff presence trebled, and the tension grew.

My continued access to higher education never felt more fragile. If Soucrer died the prison would be locked down for months, ending my access to the phone and, potentially the Programs Department. The professionals who could explain that the rising tide of violence was a reflection of draconian policy without incentives or programs no longer worked in North Carolina prisons. Or, if they did, they knew advocating for the rehabilitative idea would be interpreted as coddling criminals.

After the Soucrer incident, I could not remain silent. Too much had occurred too quickly for it not to feel connected. I understand the forces at work and witnessed how punitive reactions by prison officials always contributed to the problem. Understaffing, undertraining, and overcrowding were obvious parts of the dysfunction, but punishment without rehabilitation would never make for effective corrections. I wrote an article detailing the increased prison violence and the anti-program culture in North Carolina prisons. When *Scalawag Magazine* published "Measures Meant to make NC Prisons Safer are Doing the Opposite," my role as a reformer expanded to include a prison journalist.

Toward the end of June, Kyle mentioned the upcoming Ohio Academic Advising Association (OHAAA) Conference and invited me to co-present with her on the topic of advising correctional education (CE) students. We often discussed academic advising. Kyle was a great mentor and friend, instrumental in my advances and advocacy. Because of her help I no longer saw limits—just endless potential. I agreed to co-present.

The OHAAA audience, like the University of North Carolina students, did not know what to expect from my call. They might have been educated professionals accustomed to dealing with students at many levels, but few CE students have ready access to a phone and fewer still on death row.

Kyle believed that, in hearing from me, advisors could better help and mentor students. If anything, I hoped to clarify the difference between the needs of CE students and what they actually receive.

"Learning in prison requires dedication to the path of higher education over everything else. It's a constant, conscious effort to avoid the many pitfalls of prison life: poor self-esteem, petty arguments, fights, gangs, drugs, harassment by staff, and little encouragement—rarely is the journey easy, and failure is the expectation. Imagine if, in the midst of that struggle, somebody cared enough to guide your steps, praise success, encourage good decisions and foster critical thinking? A mentor who can navigate the complexities of university policy, avoid stereotypes, recognize your need for guidance, and provide the right amount of positive reinforcement?"

Similar to the University of North Carolina students, the OHAAA attendants responded with a mix of interest and surprise. As before, I wanted more time to talk; there was more they needed to hear. But at least for now they were thinking about the needs of CE students in new ways. I hung up pleased with how it had gone, but ever critical of the things I could have better explained.

In September 2018, as an extension of the online audio journal www.Life-Lines.is, I was invited to speak with the Religious Coalition for a Nonviolent Durham. Because of Pastor Chris Agoranos, a co-creator of the *Life Lines Collective*, the coalition wanted to hear more from death row writers on criminal justice reform. The group, a loose collective of citizens from different faiths and professions, chose to combat community violence through inclusivity, discussion, and public protest. They often spoke out about gun violence, police brutality, jail conditions, and related public policies, but had never collaborated with anyone in prison.

People of the coalition expressed amazement at speaking with someone on death row and surprise that I sounded like a normal, right-minded human being. I told them of the national prison strike in 17 states that just occurred. North Carolina was excluded from reporting on the strike, despite prisoners at three facilities participating. The North Carolina Department of Public Safety (NCDPS) would not allow national media outlets to interview prisoners and claimed no protests took place. Local journalists reported otherwise. I explained the reasons for the strike: conditions of confinement such as overcrowding and poor medical care; a need for access to higher education and better mental health services; minimum wage for work instead of slave labor.

The Religious Coalition for a Nonviolent Durham listened intently, then asked questions about what they could do to help.

Higher education awakened me to the carceral environment's many tendrils. Awareness motivated both experimental and commonsense solutions to mass incarceration I shared in these conversations with the public. On a more fundamental level I recognized the need to articulate cogent arguments and not sound or act obtuse, tone-deaf, irresponsible, or insensitive. I had to be better than ordinary if the public was going to listen.

In between speaking engagements, I contemplated my advocacy. Defining and solving problems that affect the incarcerated felt like a natural extension of my degree program in Criminal Justice Administration. As one of a handful of prisoners challenging the penal narrative, though, I understood this made me a representative by default. While that had not been my intent—mine is not the only perspective in prison—I took it as a responsibility entrusted by others who lacked a voice. The platform, in other words, is not mine, but while standing on it I have an obligation to make the most of it.

After the Religious Coalition for a Nonviolent Durham, I prepared for Dr. Page's SOC 4106 class *Crime on TV*. We talked off and on throughout the summer and early fall about shifting trends in penology. As an expert in the field and co-author of *Breaking the Pendulum: The Long Struggle Over Criminal Justice*, Dr. Page advanced my understanding of the criminal legal system. This was an advantage in working one-on-one with instructors who knew the ins and outs of criminological research. Where I shared my personal experiences with their students and presented context to the things they learned, I also learned things not usually covered in undergraduate criminology courses. Dr. Page's students, like others, were naturally curious about life on death row.

"Maybe you buy into the stereotype that we're all diabolical monsters and evil psychopaths. That we don't have families and are incapable of loving, grieving, longing, learning, or wishing our lives had been different. Not human at all. It is easier to exterminate a group of people when you believe the worst things about them, denigrating and devaluing their humanity because of the false belief people in prison are the sum of their crimes.

"Accepting this belief, laying down to die and succumbing to the oppressive weight of the death sentence is what many believe of us. The alternative is a radical act of defiance that says: I am more than a label. More than my worst mistakes. I refuse to give in to despair. Thriving as you fight death depends on your desire to live, where you place your faith and the recognition you cannot do it alone. My friends on death row are like family. Being abandoned by the world breeds understanding of one another's loss and pain. We share the same loneliness, shame, fear, uncertainty, and regrets. This strengthens our bonds as a community and makes every execution a harrowing experience."

It's not just an ability to write that enabled me to convey these experiences. The desire to help others recognize prisoners as flawed people in need of help comes from a deep sense of purpose. Prison taught me how to finesse limited resources; higher education showed me how to hone and direct them. This manifested in every published essay and speaking engagement and in the surprise of people whose preconceived notions and misconceptions I had challenged.

In the spring of 2019, Dr. Cox arranged for me to address her SOC 4950 class, *The Death Penalty in the United States*. The students read two of my unpublished essays, *Learning to Die* and *Teaching to Live* about life on death row and higher education in prison. Like I had for Dr. Baumgartner, I responded to student questions about these essays in a formal speech for the first 15-minute phone call then in the second engaged in an open Q & A that would become the format for many future engagements.

Ultimately, it always came back to higher education. How did it happen? Why would I need a degree in prison? How had it changed me? The answers were embedded in my advocacy and writing and newfound connectivity with the public. But it began with a desire to learn and offer of a single correspondence course ...

"The year I received my associate degree, I knew my life could never be the same. The words 'imperative' and 'duty' entered my thoughts. Like, 'I have a duty to use my education for more than self-gratification,' and 'It's imperative the public understand higher learning is essential to rehabilitation in prison.' Because having a degree on death row is an anomaly, it requires I strive beyond the constraints of my environment to challenge the narrative told about people in prison and on death row. I advocate for all those who want to learn and lack the resources or ability. I create greater awareness about criminal justice reform because my peace of mind rests in knowing I lived my second life as I should have the first."

14

NETWORKING

On several occasions, I asked Kyle whether it would be possible to retake *Business Law*. Prior to enrolling in new courses, she checked with the assistant dean, department chair, and ombuds office.

"They agreed you could take BUSL 2000," she told me, "And it will replace your grade from BUSL 255. It's essentially the same course. A better grade will raise your GPA."

A "better grade" had to be an A to raise my GPA above a 3.5. This would make me scholarship competitive and eligible for Departmental Honors upon graduation. Though I would have to write an honors thesis to qualify, and no CE student had ever done so, I fantasized about the "Cum Laude" designation on my degree.

Much had changed since my first time in *Business Law*. This time it would not be course credit by examination. With a better understanding of legal jargon, memorization techniques, and the benefit of graded lessons, a mid-term and final exam, I maintained an A throughout the course. Two exams limited how much I had to memorize. On the final I was even able to explain promissory estoppel in the essay portion. When the course report came back with an A-, I was ecstatic.

Satisfaction over correcting this academic flaw drove my interest toward the OU internship program. Though not required, BSS students are encouraged to seek an internship or special project that provides experiential credit for their degree. My "work" would be writing for publication since this was the one thing I could do from prison.

Within the last few years over a dozen of my essays had been published. Also, as a recent side project, I contributed writing to *Crimson Letters: Voices from Death Row*. The collection of essays by four death row co-authors was put

DOI: 10.4324/9781003449454-18

together by Tessie Castillo, who led a journaling group in the early days of Dr. K's programs. Tessie wrote to some of us and proposed a collaborative project with no guarantee of publication but at least a decent shot. With that in mind, I turned my attention back to school, prison journalism, and public speaking.

For the internship my writing would analyze the impact of public policy in correctional contexts. Penal policy had governed my life since adolescence. I knew more about its limitations and failures than many people working in the prison system. Turning that experience into expertise meant critiquing policy applications through an academic lens, then generating reports worthy of publication in criminology or political science journals. I talked with Dr. Baumgartner about the internship, and he agreed to act as my supervisor. Kyle would facilitate research and coordinate with the university to ensure I met the internship's standards.

Applying for the internship and required experimental credit course should have been as simple as any other correspondence course. Kyle sent the application in June 2019. It never arrived. When I attempted to get Ms. Roberts, the new educational coordinator, to sign a course registration form, she refused.

"Mr. Mobley has to approve your courses. When he does, I'll sign and mail the form."

No one ever needed to approve which courses, only whether I could enroll. All Ohio University CE courses are "prison safe." No advanced physics, chemistry, locksmithing, technology, or other subjects that might alarm prison officials. Up until this point, dealing with programs staff had always been a cordial, albeit drawn out, experience. Rarely did they take more than a cursory interest in my education.

"*Principles of Reasoning*? What's that?"

Roberts and Mobley, however, differed.

It began with little things.

"Show me your ID before opening the exam. Give the application to me, and I'll fill it out. Inmates don't need my contact information."

The "contact information" was her first name and NCDPS email address, both of which are on the shipping manifest and public website for the prison. Roberts spoke to Jeff (the other guy on death row taking correspondence courses) and me as if disgusted, dismissing our questions because they wasted her time, and generally treating us like children. When she left with the registration form, I hoped it wouldn't be a problem but had trouble convincing myself.

Two months passed. Roberts and Mobley (the Associate Warden of Programs) ignored letters from me and emails from Kyle asking about the registration forms. Finally, Ms. L, a programs director subordinate to Mobley, came to Unit-3 and spoke with me.

Ms. L grilled me about the internship. Roberts had the mailroom send her any mail addressed to me from the university. This kind of thing was typically only done by Internal Affairs, but even they had to notify a prisoner when mail was being inspected. Roberts seemed to think she was above such things, which explained why she had the internship application.

Arms folded, Ms. L frowned. "Why do you want a job at the prison? You can work here as staff." She twisted her face as if it was the dumbest thing she had ever heard.

"What?"

"You can't intern with NCDPS. You're an inmate."

It suddenly dawned on me what she meant. I smothered a laugh.

"If Ms. Roberts had asked me instead of taking my mail and reading it, I could have explained the internship. It's an unpaid academic internship for experiential credit. For my degree in criminal justice administration. It has nothing to do with me working in a prison. I could write three articles about the impact of draconian public policy on effective prison management, its contribution to recidivism, and how it undermines public safety."

Ms. L looked at me until I grew uncomfortable. "Well. How are you going to do that without a computer?"

Or a library with reference books. Or helpful people in programs. Some prison librarians in other states would look up information online for prisoners—not in North Carolina, which didn't even have law libraries, let alone staff who would research public records.

Instead, I said, "My advisor sends me reports and articles on new trends in the criminal legal system. The supervising professor also offered to send what I might need."

Ms. L did not particularly like the fact that I gave an immediate answer and seemed about to ask a question, then said, "We'll see," and walked off, ending the strange encounter.

My disadvantage was that correspondence courses and access to higher education was not governed by NCDPS policy. As such, my courses fell into an undefined gray area and any petty, vindictive prison official could obstruct or end them. The arbitrary justification, "we don't have enough staff to oversee this," would be used in the same way it cancelled visits, eliminated outside recreation, or neglected to deliver mail. Any excuse to avoid helping someone in prison.

Ms. L did inform me Captain H., the Support Services Manager for Central Prison, would be reviewing whether it was even legal for me to be an intern. So, I wrote to Captain H. and explained the internship at length, then sent copies of the letter to every top administrator at Central Prison. I did this to ensure everyone knew about the effort to obstruct my access to higher education and to remove any plausible deniability if it came down to a lawsuit.

Toward mid-September, Roberts called Kyle, "Good news! Mr. Mobley wants to talk to you."

Nothing about Kyle's conversation with Mobley was good. The AWOP chastised her because the internship application had a Post-It note with the words "Love, Kyle." She often did this rather than include a letter because Kyle dealt with over 50 students. Use of the word "love" offended Mobley as it had the unit manager responsible for ending Dr. K's programs.

"I need to speak with your supervisor. Your conduct is unacceptable."

Kyle tried to argue she had not violated any university or prison policy, but Mobley was adamant. "You people are wasting resources on condemned inmates. It won't be long before executions resume. What then?"

Fortunately, Joe, Kyle's supervisor, happened to be one of my former academic advisors and of a different philosophy than Mobley. Joe knew of my progress as a student and contributions to the academic advising conference. He also previously taught college-in-prison courses and was accustomed to dealing with people like Mobley.

"As long as Lyle enrolls in OU courses, abides our policies, and he isn't violating prison policy, I don't see what the problem is. Kyle's conduct isn't a problem either, but I'll have a word with her."

After Kyle related this to me, I gave Mobley a week and when no signed forms turned up at the university, I wrote a letter to the newly appointed commissioner of prisons, Todd Ishee:

> Dear Commissioner Ishee,
>
> I am writing this letter in the hope that you can resolve an ongoing problem with the pursuit of privately funded correspondence courses and degree programs by people incarcerated in North Carolina prisons.

I described the history, funding, and success of my higher education on death row, how previous wardens and programs staff had facilitated it, and the nature of my problem now. I also expressed why access to education is important, even for people on death row.

> Though I am on death row, my case is under appeal while I contest my conviction and sentence. It is entirely reasonable to believe a court may grant relief from my sentence or conviction. Since 1973 the reversal rate of death sentences on appeal in North Carolina is approximately 71–74 percent. Since then, eight people were exonerated and all of them struggled upon release because they lacked access to educational programs and rehabilitative services while on death row.
>
> It is critical I pursue any educational opportunity for whatever form of relief comes of my appeals. There are, for example, a number of degree-bearing lifers in prison who act as mentors and facilitators of programs for those who will re-enter society one day. These are two of many reasons why higher education applies as much to life in prison as it does to reentry. As a former Ohio prison warden, I believe you are aware of this.

I asked Commissioner Ishee to create a policy that removed any uncertainty the pursuit
of higher education in North Carolina prisons would be preserved as a right and encouraged by programs staff, regardless of one's custody level.

> Higher education is about personal growth and transforming one's thinking. Credentials, preparing for reentry, and becoming a productive member of the community are byproducts of that journey. This is a worthy use of one's time when so few state-funded programs exist and gangs are spreading. Considering the recent systemic failures in North Carolina prisons and your appointment in their wake, encouraging individual rehabilitative efforts is essential to changing that narrative.

I mailed copies of the letter to the Director and Regional Director of Prisons, Director of Educational Services, and the warden, hoping someone responded but not counting on it. Lyden, the director of Hidden Voices and one of Dr. K's former volunteers, grew interested in the problem when I told her the steps I had taken. She offered to contact a friend of hers in the state legislature. I sent her a copy of my degree audit report and letter to Commissioner Ishee to contextualize the obstruction, and the duration and success of my higher education on death row. Then I had to wait.

Throughout the obstruction, I continued with other writing and even made new connections for speaking events. Emily Baxter, then executive director of the North Carolina Alliance Against the Death Penalty, and founder of the non-profit We Are All Criminals, invited me to co-present with her at two events: the AmeriCorps VISTA—Minnesota Youth Alliance conference in November and St. Paul's Lutheran Church in December. Then Jennifer introduced me to Seth Kotch after I mentioned liking his book *Lethal State: A History of the Death Penalty in North Carolina*. Seth taught American studies at UNC Chapel Hill and invited me to speak with his AMST 278: *Crimes and Punishments* undergraduate class.

Like Frank Baumgartner's *Deadly Justice*, Josh Page's *Toughest Beat* and *Breaking the Pendulum*, Seth Kotch's *Lethal State* served as supplemental reading for my degree program. These books and others deepened my understanding of the sociopolitical forces influencing the criminal legal system and my life. While reading their books, I didn't think I would ever develop working relationships with the authors, but the world of academic writing on criminal justice administration is small and interconnected. Each author referenced sociologists, criminologists, and research I studied, demonstrating the importance of consensus in the social sciences, and bringing theory to life. On a much smaller scale, it lent historical perspective to my fight for higher education and need for resilience.

Unwilling to remain idle during the obstruction, I wrote two articles about the obstacles to higher education in prison. It wasn't enough to write letters easily ignored by prison officials or hope a friend of a friend would make some inquiries on my behalf. In a television interview, the commissioner had stated support for improving the mental well-being of people in prison. I intended to call him out on it and increase public awareness of one potential solution. *Scalawag* had agreed to publish *Obstructing Reform: Obstacles to Higher Education in Prison*, and InsideHigherEd.com would publish *Resilience and Resistance: The Fight for Higher Education in Prison*.

I didn't know if my efforts would work. Prison officials get away with human rights violations as long as no court, lawmaker, governor, or media hold them accountable. I witnessed this in 2017. It was only after investigative reporting and the death of five prison staff that the legislature really bothered to pay attention to the failures of North Carolina prisons. I could only try my best to convince people that draconian tough-on-crime policies are the cause of those failures and why access to higher education is a better path. If nothing else, I was equipped for the fight and believed in the right to education. No one could take that from me.

Concession came almost six months after the obstruction began.

A short brown-haired woman form the Programs Department had me summoned to the office. "Give me your course registration form so I can get it signed and mailed." She held her hand out, palm up, as if expecting payment for a debt. I stared as if she spoke another language, so she repeated it slowly and sarcastically.

"Bring. Me. Your. Forms. To. Sign. All of them."

"Does this mean I can do the internship?"

"No. It means you can continue with your courses."

"Where's Ms. Roberts?"

"Around, but on her way out. I'm just her gopher for now."

Relieved, I smiled, "And Mobley?"

"Still here. Are you gonna get those forms or what?"

Victory is an exhilarating experience. In retrospect, the six-month battle was not long, but it would have ended my degree program if I chose to do nothing. It never mattered that I obey the rules and am a good student. Two petty prison bureaucrats decided they disliked someone on death row finding empowerment through education and tried to stop it. They couldn't have anticipated the depth of my understanding of how bureaucracies work, how much education means to me, or the number of people ready to help me. Networking matters. Belief in higher education really matters. Commitment to the journey matters the most.

EPILOGUE

I had hoped my alma mater Ohio University would expand the course selection for their print based Correctional Education (CE) program. With only a half dozen courses left to complete my bachelor's degree, I didn't want to simply fill those spots with whatever sociology courses were left in a depleted course catalog for incarcerated students.

My hope of a better selection was reasonable since the 2020 FAFSA Simplification Act completely restored access to Pell Grants for all prisoners. More federal funds for prospective students should have meant higher enrollment and more print based courses. Except, it did not. The return of Pell Grants for the incarcerated drove some Ohio University administrators to seek an end to the CE program amidst other cuts which impacted the program during the 2020–2021 school year.

In 2020 Ohio University, which serves rural BIPOC and rural white communities, began laying off faculty and staff and furloughing administrative staff in departments across the university due to expectations of declining enrollment. Several language programs were eliminated, and instructional faculty from a variety of disciplines received notifications that their contracts would not be renewed. Despite these cuts and concerns about declining enrollment, OU enrolled record-breaking freshman classes in both 2022 and 2023. In a discussion with a recent graduate of OU, who on social media organized grassroots protests over the faculty cuts, the student expressed outrage over what she perceived as political decisions by the university.

"There was a lot of anger and disbelief amongst students who felt betrayed by their school. It was completely blatant, callous, and unnecessary."

In 2022, I reached the rank of senior. It had been a battle to get this far because of increased resistance to higher education amongst some Central

DOI: 10.4324/9781003449454-19

Prison administrators. For several years I struggled to maintain access to college correspondence courses even after securing the 2020 scholarship from the Alpha Sigma Lambda Honor Society. Being this close to the finish line of such an impossible journey over 15 years in the making lent every small advance a big sense of accomplishment. It also meant I knew what to do to maintain my access to higher education no matter what obstacles were erected.

The decision to pursue an associate degree through OU was a major turning point in my life, one that signaled a commitment to higher education in an environment hostile to it. Earning a degree was an extension of my dedication and a renewed sense of responsibility to use my education in a way that benefits my peers and the community. As a writer, and ultimately an incarcerated journalist, I found myself obligated to provide greater context and insight on how the criminal legal system continues to oppress the marginalized and undermine public safety. Because what I write is an extension of how I learned, I can back up my arguments and observations with documented research and scholarship of the experts who came before me and add in my own experience as illustration. I can, as journalist Medhi Hasan says, "show the receipts."

I know well what it means to withstand an assault on education. At some point it grows difficult to deny the existence of anti-intellectualism, but especially when it functions as false morality that undermines higher learning, whitewashes history, bans books on identity and culture, and demonizes diversity. Ohio University may succumb to that problem; the state is considering passage of SB 83, which limits the ability to teach about diversity, gender, and sexuality. However, Ohio is not alone, or even the most adversely impacted by such efforts. West Virginia is eliminating 169 faculty positions and more than 30 degree programs from its primary university. Like OU, it is cutting language programs under the guise of budgetary necessity. Administrators at West Virginia University, and universities in Missouri, Kansas, and Virginia worked with the GOP backed RPK Group to reduce and remove the influence of liberal arts programs, which includes humanities that teach critical thinking, history, literature, and philosophy, but also math and sciences. More blatant attacks on diversity and inclusion are occurring in Florida, with SB 266, and Texas, with Bill 17. These efforts undermine public education through a type of gerrymandering that forces the ideas of diversity and equality into more elite institutions, and further disadvantages the poor by entrenching the divide between white America and everyone else.

Though Ohio University has yet to fall off of that particular cliff, in August 2023, a month after the official return of Pell Grants for the incarcerated, the school decided to end the oldest college correspondence course degree program in the US. Their reasons, published in a FAQ sheet released by the Office of Continuing Education, are:

1. lower interest in correspondence courses
2. changes in access to federal funding for programs at other institutions
3. increased digital access to remote areas formerly served by correspondence programs

It's unlikely anyone at the Office of Continuing Education or OU at large bothered to survey who is interested in taking a college correspondence course. Equally unlikely is that they queried DOC directors about becoming a Pell approved prison education program (PEP), as is required by the FAFSA Simplification Act. What likely happened is that whoever made the decision to cut the CE program was only interested in online student enrollment, which did increase during the pandemic, but has absolutely nothing to do with anyone in prison. The "remote areas" formerly served by correspondence courses is a reference to military personnel and the shift to online enrollment. And while, yes, there has been a big change in federal funding with increased access to Pell Grants, and yes, more universities will offer PEPs as they did in the 80s and 90s, this does not justify ending the CE program.

Had it not been for the standards of university accreditation, it is unlikely those responsible for ending Ohio University's nearly 50-year-old college correspondence program for the incarcerated would have cared whether current students were able to finish their degree program. Thankfully, accreditation requires that a closing university, or one making decisions to cut programs, has to "teach out" enrolled students. OU will have to accommodate incarcerated students in active degree programs to ensure they are able to finish. It is a small concession.

I was neither surprised nor unprepared by the end of the CE program. I had already planned to transfer to Adams State University to take advantage of their advanced paralegal courses to round out my degree. But there were also other frustrating problems that prompted my transfer: the pandemic made the university mailroom unreliable, and lessons were frequently lost; the testing center misplaced exams on multiple occasions; the turnaround on graded lessons often took months. I knew that to progress change was necessary. I knew it was better to function independently of an institution instead of being a slave to it. My education from, and experience with, Ohio University as an incarcerated student taught me that and much, much more.

AFTERWORD

Lyle May has revealed to us a view of his life as a student, scholar, and advocate. He played all these roles while incarcerated and with the deprivations that come with this experience. May has discussed his need for an educational journey, one to enrich his life and fill his yearning for knowledge. Furthermore, this book offers the audience insight into May's desire, devotion, and labors to advocate for prisoners' rights to education as a means for healing, rehabilitation, and chances for personal and social success.

Barriers Faced by Returning Citizens

Every year hundreds of thousands of people leave American correctional institutions to return to their lives in society (Jonson & Cullen, 2015; Petersilia, 2009). Many of them are ready, and hopeful, to be productive as contributing members of the workforce, effective parents, and accepted back by family members and community neighbors. Hopes and bonds can only carry a person so far if they are faced with difficulty finding viable and stable employment. When returning citizens are cut off from gainful employment, chances of acquiring safe and affordable housing diminish (McKernan, 2017). These challenges become even more difficult to overcome if educational programming was deficient and inaccessible during a person's incarceration.

May has offered the reader a glimpse into the struggles that he and others face during incarceration, struggles that are especially influential for incarcerated folks serving lengthy and life sentences. Concurring issues such as substance use disorders (SUDs), mental and physical health illnesses/disorders, and impacts of trauma occur for many while trying to navigate the system to

DOI: 10.4324/9781003449454-20

gain access to educational programs. As such, prisons should offer people support and resources needed to rehabilitate during their incarceration.

Improvements for Future Accessibility of Education Programming Inside Correctional Facilities

May has provided numerous examples (from his perspective as a student and a correctional reform advocate) as to how prison educational programs have been operated efficiently and inefficiently. He has covered the rewards and disappointments he has experienced as a participant. Furthermore, he has critically examined and discussed practices and policies that have worked to the detriment of correctional education programs. Examining the opposite of these practices may demonstrate to policymakers, correctional administrators, and the public how correctional programs could be implemented in a more efficient and beneficial manner to incarcerated people.

Moving Forward

Education can be an effective tool to help set incarcerated people on a positive path to restore their place as contributing citizens of our society. The knowledge gained from correctional education programs will likely assist many people to develop the insight and skills needed to keep from returning to prison, by enhancing job marketability, development of cognitive functioning, and contributing to the growth of skills such as communication and discipline, in turn, preventing further financial drain on taxpayers. Decades of policies leading to mass incarceration have focused on "bars and guards" to address society's crime problems. It is now time to shift that ideology to put policies in place that build classrooms and distribute educational resources to prisoners who are dedicated to the betterment of themselves and their communities.

Lisa M. Carter, Ph.D.

References

Jonson, C. L., & Cullen, F. T. (2015). Prisoner reentry programs. *Crime and Justice*, 44(1), 517–575.

McKernan, P. (2017). Homelessness and prisoner reentry: Examining barriers to housing stability and evidence-based strategies that promote improved outcomes. *Journal of Community Corrections*, 27(1), 1–14.

Petersilia, J. (2009). *When Prisoners Come Home: Parole and Prisoner Reentry*. Oxford University Press.

References

Barkow, R. E. (2019). *Prisoners of Politics: Breaking the Cycle of Mass Incarceration*. Harvard University Press.

Bartollas, C., & Schmalleger, F. (2014). *Juvenile Delinquency* (9th ed.). Pearson.

Becker, H. (1963). *Outsiders: Studies in Sociology of Deviance*. The Free Press.

Chestnut, K., & Wachendorfer, A. (2021, April). Second chance Pell: Four years of expanding access to education in prisons. The Vera Institute. www.vera.org/publica tions/second-chance-pell-four-years-of-expanding-access- to-education-in-prison.

Fagan, F., & Piquero, A. R. (2007). Rational choice and developmental influences on recidivism among adolescent felony offenders. *Journal of Empirical Legal Studies*, 4, 715–748.

FAFSA Simplification Act, Division FF, Title VII, U.S. Department of Education. Consolidated Appropriations Act (2021). 116th U.S. Congress.

Feeley, M. M., & Simon, J. (1992). The new penology: Notes on the emerging strategy of corrections and its implications. *Criminology*, 30(4), 449–474. doi:10.1111/j.1745–9125.1992.tb01112.x.

Frailing, K., & Harper, Jr., D. W. (2019). The social construction of deviance, conflict, and the criminalization of midwives, New Orleans: 1940s and 1950s. *Deviant Behavior*, 31(8), 729–755. doi:10.1080/01639620903416073.

Gibney, B. C. (2019). *The Nonsense Factory: The Making and Breaking of the American Legal System*. Hatchell Books.

Johnson, R., Rocheleau, A. M., & Martin, A. B. (2017). *Hard Time* (4th ed.). Wiley-Blackwell.

Kappeler, V. E., & Potter, G. W. (2018). *The Mythology of Crime and Criminal Justice* (5th ed.). Waveland Press.

Krieghbaum, A. (2019, July 16). Full repeal of the Pell ban in prisons top of mind at annual convening of Second Chance pilot. *Inside Higher Ed*. www.insidehighered.com/news/2019/07/16/full-repeal-pell-ban-prisons-topmind- annual-convening-second-chance-pilot.

Leyva, M., & Bickel, C. (2010) For corrections to college: The value of a convict's voice. *Western Criminology Review*, 11(1), 50–59.

Martinez-Hill, J. (2021). A monumental shift: Restoring access to Pell Grants for incarcerated students. The Vera Institute. www.vera.org/downloads/publications/restoring-access-to-pell-grants-for-incarcerated-students.pdf.

Mooney, J. (2020). *The Theoretical Foundations of Criminology: Place, Time, and Context*. Routledge.

Newbold, G., Ross, J. I., Jones, R. S., Richards, S. C., & Lenza, M. (2014). Prison research from the inside: The role of convict autoethnography. *Qualitative Inquiry*, 20(4), 439–448. https://doi.org/10.1177/1077800413516269.

Page, J. (2004). Eliminating the enemy: The import of denying prisoners access to higher education in Clinton's America. *Punishment and Society*, 6(4), 357–378. https://doi.org/10.1177/1462474504046118.

Pettit, E. (2019, January 16). Ending the ban on Pell Grants for prisoners is said to yield "cascade of benefits". *The Chronicle of Higher Education*. www.chronicle.com/article/ending-ban-on-pell-grants-for-prisoners-is-said-to-yield-cascade-of-benefits/.

Pratt, J. (2007). *Penal Populism*. Routledge.

Roberts, J. V., Stalans, L. S., Indermaur, D., & Hough, M. (2003). *Penal Populism and Public Opinion: Lessons from Five Countries*. Oxford University Press.

Ross, J. I., & Richards, S. C. (2003). *Convict Criminology*. Wadsworth Publishing.

Tannenbaum, F. (1938). *Crime and Community*. Columbia University Press.

Turk, A. (1969). *Criminality and Legal Order*. Rand-McNally.

UN Survey on Crime trends and operations of criminal justice systems, Office of Drugs and Crime. Prisoners and incarcerations rates in selected countries.

West, C. (2021, December 14). So what's happening with Pell? *College Inside*. Open Campus Media.

INDEX